PARENTING CHILDREN WITH ADHD

A Comprehensive Guide for Parents with Fun Activities to Help Your Child Develop Their Skills and Reach Their Full Potential!

SAMANTHA HANKINS

INTRODUCTION TO ADHD IN CHILDREN

When the time comes to learn tips, techniques, and expert advice on your own on how to help your child from the moment they've been diagnosed with attention deficit hyperactivity disorder (ADHD), it's necessary to have a guide or a helping hand that can support you in these difficult moments.

That is why this book is dedicated to you, who thinks that the world is closing in on you and you don't know what to do in such a situation. The truth is that you may be panicking because you think it is something that is beyond you, but it is not.

Just look around you and stop to observe that all people, no matter how small or inconspicuous, live with a condition, be it physical, psychological, emotional, social, economic, or cultural, among others.

The issue here is the great concern that overwhelms you as a parent, and it is completely understandable because a parent always wants to give their best to their children and wants to see them happy and will do whatever it takes to make them happy.

A Normal Life

It is common that before a diagnosis of attention deficit hyperactivity disorder, you think that your child will not lead a normal life, but: What is a normal life? This can have several perspectives from whoever sees it. Let me tell you that what is normal for you may not be for others.

Certainly, your child may develop or exhibit behavioral or temperament problems due to their condition. However, the good thing is that there are techniques that can help your child achieve their goals in life, whether in the family group, in school, or in social life in general.

You will be one of those in charge and possibly the one with the greatest responsibility for this to happen. For this reason, below we present the tools and knowledge that you should take into account since there are many studies that have currently been dedicated to demonstrating how a certain lifestyle can be carried out with children with ADHD.

Here you will find practical suggestions and answers to those situations that, no matter how complex they may seem to you, are common in people with ADHD. Are you willing to learn about ADHD in detail? Well, here's a guide to doing it the right way, in the most enjoyable way possible, without the need for in-depth study to treat your child.

The important thing is that you understand from now on that your child is not disabled and that you should not make them feel sick. They are a member of your life, a valuable ally from whom you also have to learn.

You are not alone, because there are many parents and family members who are trying different strategies to use them in an ADHD lifestyle.

This book takes a tour of the essentials, about what the disorder really is, how it manifests itself, details about the diagnosis, studies and other disorders that can be similar to ADHD, the causes, factors that affect its development, the emotions of the children with ADHD, and the best advice for you and for them. Begin to know this world. I will accompany you!

CHAPTER 1

ADHD DIAGNOSIS AND SYMPTOMS

The first stop on this tour begins by learning what attention deficit hyperactivity disorder (ADHD) means and its symptoms. Something that is necessary to understand since from this, you can begin to identify many characteristic events that surely occur daily and you still do not understand how to interpret them.

The important thing is that you recognize how ADHD works and thus take charge of the situation. It is possible that in your mind you have some idea of what is happening, but you are not sure, so it is advisable to take this knowledge and techniques seriously to adequately address your child's condition.

This Is How ADHD Is Defined

Attention deficit hyperactivity disorder (ADHD) is known as a neurobiological disorder that ends up triggering changes in the child's learning and behavior.

To make it a little more explicit, the neurobiological alteration refers to diseases that originate from the central and peripheral nervous system, the brain, the spinal cord, the cranial and peripheral nerves, the autonomic nervous system, the nerve roots, the neuromuscular junction, and the muscles.

It is considered a very common psychiatric difficulty in childhood and has become the most frequent reason for child psychiatry consultation, so you should not be scared or alarmed, as it is a situation that you can see in many other people, families, or even relatives.

This condition is more common in boys. It is believed to be 9% more common in boys than in girls (3.3%). The first thing you usually see in these children is that they develop attention problems, impulsivity, and an insatiable desire to be active. Experts say that because of these symptoms, difficulties in social interaction and school performance develop.

Another detail that you will see later is that they are usually associated with other problems such as oppositional defiant disorder, depression, conduct disorder, and anxiety.

Reaching the conclusion and determining if a child has attention deficit hyperactivity disorder (ADHD) requires a process that consists of several steps, and of which you will know in this book to be able to apply them.

The truth is that there is no single test to diagnose this condition because there are a variety of problems such as anxiety, depression, and certain types of learning disorders that can present similar symptoms and from which you must learn to differentiate them.

If you're worried that your child may have ADHD, the first step is to talk to a healthcare professional who can help you determine if the symptoms your child is experiencing are consistent with the disorder.

You should also keep in mind that the diagnosis can be made by a mental health professional such as a psychiatrist, psychologist, primary care worker, or even a pediatrician because, as you will see, the help landscape begins to expand in this period; that is, there are several professionals who can help you.

For its part, the American Academy of Pediatrics (AAP), one of the first institutions that parents usually go to, recommends that pediatricians ask parents, teachers, and other adults who are in charge of the child about their conduct. Normally they tend to question those who care for the child in different contexts, such as the home, at school or any other place where they frequently attend.

In addition, the ADHD professional must also determine if the child has another conditioning characteristic that may better explain the symptoms, or that occurs along with ADHD.

These Are the Ways How to Diagnose ADHD

Healthcare professionals in psychiatric specialties have the guidelines of the Diagnostic and Statistical Manual (DSM-5), which has five editions (each updated with various parameters) and is endorsed by the American Psychiatric Association to diagnose ADHD.

It is precisely this pattern of diagnosis that is one of the most used to help ensure that the diagnosis and treatment of children with ADHD are carried out correctly. The practice of this form of diagnosis is also used to help determine the number of children who have ADHD and the public health impact of this disorder.

It is based on a series of criteria that it is important that you have just to expand your knowledge since you must remember that it is not up to you to make a diagnosis. The idea is that parents know the scenario from the root and knowing how a diagnosis is made is part of it. Although healthcare providers are trained to diagnose or treat ADHD, you need to understand the following information.

Children with ADHD exhibit persistent behavior that results in inattentiveness, hyperactivity, or impulsivity, which in turn is so extreme that it interferes with the functioning or development of:

Attention Impairment

The way to diagnose is based on checking six or more symptoms of inattention in children up to 16 years of age, or five or more for adolescents 17 years of age or older and also adults. You should know that these symptoms of inattention must have manifested for about 6 months:

- Commonly does not pay due attention to detail or makes careless mistakes in school, work, or other activities.
- Generally has difficulty sustaining attention on tasks or activities that are recreational.
- Usually does not listen when spoken to directly.
- Frequently fails to comply with instructions and does not complete school activities, as well as household chores or work responsibilities, ie, loses concentration or wanders.
- Often has difficulty organizing tasks and activities.
- Often avoids or feels uncomfortable or refuses to perform tasks that require mental effort for a long period of time, this usually occurs in school activities or homework.
- It is common to lose utensils necessary for tasks and activities, such as school supplies, books, pencils, tools, wallets, keys, papers, glasses, cell phones, or other devices.
- Is easily distracted.
- Forgets things while doing daily activities.

The Criterion of Hyperactivity and Impulsivity

This criterion is widely named and perhaps one of the most marked aspects. Professionals in charge of the diagnosis usually rely on six or more symptoms of hyperactivity or impulsivity criteria for children up to 16 years of age, or five or more for adolescents 17 years of age and older and also in adults.

Indeed, the symptoms of hyperactivity or impulsivity must have been present for at least 6 months to the point that they are detrimental and inappropriate for the person's level of development:

- Frequently acts nervously or taps hands or feet, as well as squirms in the seat.
- Generally leaves chair in situations where remaining seated is expected.
- Starts to run or climb in situations in which it is not appropriate, in the case of adolescents or adults it can be limited to a feeling of restlessness.
- Cannot play or participate in recreational activities in a quiet manner.
- Is in constant motion and acts as if it has a running engine.

- Commonly overexpresses or talks.
- Tends to blurt out an answer before finishing asking a question.
- Often has trouble waiting their turn.
- Constantly interrupts others or intrudes on conversations or games.

To these symptoms that appeared before the age of 12, the fulfillment of these conditions is added:

- Some of the symptoms developed in two or more contexts, such as in activities at home, school, or work, or with friends and family, such as in everyday life.
- There are clear indications that the symptoms interfere with social, school, and work functioning, and that its quality is also affected.
- The symptoms occur without any explanation and are associated with another mental disorder, such as a mood disorder, anxiety disorder, dissociative disorder, or personality disorder. The symptoms do not occur during episodes of schizophrenia or another psychotic disorder.

Another perspective that is presented as a way of evaluating is the types of symptoms, and these present themselves in three types of ADHD:

Combined Exposure

One way to assess is whether enough or most of the symptoms of both criteria—inattention and hyperactivity/impulsivity—occurred during the last six months.

Manifestation in Which Inattention Predominates

If most or enough of the symptoms of inattention, but not hyperactivity or impulsivity, occurred in the past six months.

Manifestation in Which Hyperactivity or Impulsivity Prevails

If there were enough symptoms of hyperactivity or impulsivity, but not of inattention, in the last six months. Since the symptoms can change over time, the manifestation can also change over time.

These Are the Early Warning Signs of ADHD

Although you previously knew what specialists evaluate in a diagnosis, it is necessary that as a mother you understand that there are signs that you should pay attention to. Most experts agree that the tendency to develop ADHD is present from birth, although ADHD symptoms are often not noticed until children start elementary school.

This is because almost all preschool children frequently show ADHD behaviors or symptoms such as inattention, impulsive and hyperactive behaviors, behaviors that are often seen as part of their normal development. While other children progressively stop such behaviors. Children with this disorder, on the other hand, do not leave them and this difference is increasingly noticeable as they grow older.

It is necessary to pay attention to the school stage because it is the space where a child's problems associated with inattention, impulsivity, and hyperactivity can be highlighted since class activities require a greater amount of concentration, tolerance, and self-control. These types of demands are not as prevalent at home or in playgroups, so it is in these contexts that one can see if the child could have had fewer problems.

It is common that by the time a child with this disorder reaches the age of seven, their parents are able to be aware that their child's inattention, activity level, or impulsivity is becoming more evident than is typical.

After reading this information, you may have noticed that your child has had some of these symptoms for some time, such as being almost unable to concentrate on a book, reading, or doing homework for a short period of time even if you are there to help them.

You may have also noticed that they feel exhausted at the end of the day and are too active as if they were still 2 years old.

It is also common for children with this condition to ask you questions so frequently that you have begun to suspect that this is not common for them, or you may have noticed that your child does not seem to grasp the subtleties of relationships with others, such as respecting the personal space of others, allowing other people to have their turn to speak during a conversation, something that their playmates have begun to adopt.

I know that it is common for some mothers to say that this type of behavior is just part of the normal process of growing up. When they are problematic, they also say that it is normal due to parenting difficulties, as it is also customary to justify the temperament of their child with the thought: "They are only children with a difficult character," and so many justifications arise that do not really go to the extreme of thinking that it is a disorder like ADHD.

That is why, in order to diagnose a child with the disorder, what is advisable in the case of pediatricians is that they manage to gather information about the child's behavior, at least in an environment other than the home environment, this includes an examination report prepared by teachers and school professionals.

It is with this that the behavior of a child from two or more environments can be compared. A specialist establishes differences between such reasons that are presented for attention problems such as the common: "They have a difficult temperament but that is normal", ineffective parenting practices, inappropriate academic environment, and other challenges.

Also, they can clarify whether the child's behavior is preventing them from functioning adequately in more than one environment, another detail that is presented as a requirement for diagnosis.

This Is What You Notice When ADHD Behaviors Arise

It is often difficult to accept behavior that you see in your child that matches the formal terms used by pediatricians and other medical professionals.

You rarely think that your child may have hyperactivity and impulsivity problems, as is the case with parents who normalize such behavior. Yes, it's common for you to think: "Why can't my child sit still?"

The truth is that in order not to confuse the picture, the terms that doctors use for these behaviors have changed in recent years. In case you didn't know, the term "ADHD" was used earlier and mainly referred to the form of ADHD with symptoms like "inattention."

Under this term, the parents certainly did not have an idea of how important it was to know about this whole situation since these children are not very active and their symptoms can go unnoticed by many adults because it is simply not disturbing. Later, however, the general term "ADHD" came to be used typically when describing all types of ADHD in a more specific way.

It is when you go through the list of typical behavi⬚ with ADHD, that you ask yourself as a mother ab⬚ day or week that your child says or thinks the same ⬚ fact that mothers ask such questions from time to time.

In contrast, in the case of parents of children with ADHD, they continue to observe the same behaviors daily and for long periods, long after their classmates and other children their age have already progressed.

Not All Children Show Symptoms

Children with ADHD may have one or more of the above types of symptoms; however, not all manifest in the same way. The symptoms are usually frequent in some and not in others.

Integrated Brain Attentional Procedures in ADHD

When you look at the behavior of children with this condition, you see that they make mistakes in these areas and have difficulty performing most of these actions.

It is possible that your curiosity here becomes more important and you wonder what are the failures that occur and where it occurs, so you should know that the underlying brain functioning of those with ADHD is characterized by developing less functional activity and a smaller size in this area responsible for these actions.

To be more explicit, you should know that previously when this disorder was defined, it was done based on the fact that it was a disease that originates from the central and peripheral nervous system of the brain.

These being so, you should know that the brain has special circuits for each of its different functions and these are the attention circuits that are in the cerebral cortex of the frontal zone. This part is known as the area called prefrontal, which controls working memory, attention, and thus the inhibition of responses.

On the other hand, there is the fact that in children with ADHD, the circuits and groups of neurons that control attention are smaller and less active, also known as neural hypofunction.

It happens that in people with ADHD, when this deficient function occurs in these circuits, the brain compensates by activating other emotional zones or motor zones, generating defective data processing.

Attention Control

Putting your attention on a task, selecting the important parts, locating possible problems, attending to details, and inhibiting distracting elements that take you away from the objective or goal to finally achieve the successful completion of a task depends on a person's ability.

This attention is divided into domains based on the object of attention and the attentional response or the degree or level of attention of the person. The truth is that each domain of attention has its function and importance when carrying out a task, and each action or task requires one type of attention or another.

Alert Status

Alertness is the ability to be awake and stay alert. It is the physiological activation of the organism. It works as a primary activation response and is activated by a very noticeable, attractive, novel stimulus or by a dangerous situation. In addition, it involves the ability to follow stimuli or orders.

Focused Attention

It refers to the ability that helps you to be focused on a visual, auditory, or tactile stimulus. Here the fixation time to the stimulus is not valued, but the ability you have to redirect the attentional focus towards the correct stimulus.

Sustained Attention

This is the ability to maintain a response consistently for a long time. It has two subcomponents and one of them refers to being vigilant when the task is to detect a stimulus and concentration when it refers to other cognitive tasks.

Sustained attention is directly related to working memory, especially in tasks that involve the maintenance and manipulation of information actively in the mind, ranging from mathematical operations to calculation, and management of alternatives.

Selective Attention

Selective attention is where you can notice more failures since it is characterized by the ability to select something among several possible ones. It works when you want to process relevant information or the appropriate action scheme, inhibiting attention to some stimuli while attending to others.

When there is ADHD, this attention is simply not met adequately resulting in numerous distractions, either by external or internal stimuli.

Changing Attention

This type of attention refers to the ability of an individual to allow changing the focus of attention between tasks that require certain different cognitive requirements, controlling what data is processed at each moment.

When ADHD is present, this process is simply truncated, not being able to alternate attention when you must pay attention to more than one stimulus.

Divided Attention

It refers to the ability to pay attention to two things at the same time. This is very common in your day to day, as it is the ability of a person to make the selection of more than one piece of information at the same time or of more than one process or action scheme simultaneously. It is the process that allows the distribution of our resources.

Once you understand how your brain and its attentional system work, you have a starting point, more knowledge about how this type of attention is fulfilled in your child, and in your other children, since the age comparison allows you to see and locate yourself more easily in the scenario where they are.

I know that many mothers sometimes require more and more tests because it is difficult to understand this, but simply inform yourself and observe. Do not allow these details to pass by before your eyes or that you end up confusing them with others, like the ones that we will discuss in the next chapter.

CHAPTER 2

CONDITIONS THAT ARE CONFUSED WITH ADHD

Based on the fact that out of every three ADHD diagnoses, one is incorrect, it is necessary that you also know that there are other conditions similar to these. Therefore, from the beginning emphasis has been placed on the idea of being informed and knowing. In this chapter, you will find a list of similar conditions.

In the last chapter, everything about ADHD and its telltale symptoms became clear, as well as a series of implications that occur in the brain that affect the attention system. It is very important to be clear about this information to know what happens in your child's little brain and thus understand the following processes. Remember that it is not your responsibility to make a diagnosis, but you do need to be aware of everything that happens with them since when you go to a consultation or involve them in a group, you are the best person to explain and prepare others around them about their condition.

This Is What the Studies Say

You must understand that the constant studies referring to ADHD have focused on carefully studying its origin and development so that parents can know and thereby prepare themselves together with their children, because here the idea is to act as a team and that their child is not treated as a sick person since this is not the case.

Important: You should know that the most recent studies carried out by North American psychiatrists have shown that 34% of ADHD diagnoses are incorrect. It is a situation of overdiagnosis that is caused by the current systems to diagnose ADHD.

These, in turn, are based exclusively on the clinical history provided by parents, relatives, and educators, as well as on the evaluation of the patient themselves, which is always associated with a certain degree of subjectivity, both on the part of the informants and the evaluators. Here is the importance as a parent or guardian of knowing and identifying what is happening with your child.

False Positives

The context discussed above leads to a high degree of false positives, that is, cases diagnosed with ADHD without really being so and that ADHD ends up being confused with behaviors that are normal to a certain extent in childhood, such as impulsivity or inattention, or also that the diagnoses are confused with other pathologies such as alterations in the development of language and learning, obsessive-compulsive symptoms, dyslexia, dyspraxia, anxiety disorders, depression, and even psychosis.

Other diagnoses can be confused with sleep disorders, Tourette syndrome, epileptic disorders, thyroid disorders, or side effects of drugs.

In most cases, behavior patterns that occur simply at a lower degree of psychomotor development of the child are taken as indicative of ADHD. For example, some studies show how, within the same school group, the probability of being diagnosed with ADHD is greater in younger children, given that their birthday falls on the dates immediately after the deadline for schooling.

The truth is that given this panorama and to reduce this high percentage of false positives, many institutes dedicated to ADHD have developed a new system that, in addition to the usual clinical evaluation, also includes the performance of a quantitative electroencephalogram (qEEG), which calculates the Brain Function Index using biomarkers that provide objective data allowing the doctor to confirm or rule out in 90% of cases if the child really has ADHD.

The tests carried out on children already clinically diagnosed with ADHD last between 20 and 30 minutes, and consist of the application of various electrodes to the head. This is another way to diagnose and is based on a quantitative calculation in the electroencephalogram (EEG).

The truth is that a correct diagnosis is essential because, in the treatment of ADHD, psychotropic drugs are used that may be justified in this condition, but that administered to healthy children or with other pathologies can be dangerous, especially when at this age the brain tissue is in full development phase.

Therefore, you have to be careful and inform yourself about all the processes that exist to do it adequately and that it yields the results you expect, but above all, that it is not a trauma for them.

Other Problems and Disorders With ADHD

ADHD commonly co-occurs with other disorders, and approximately half of the children diagnosed have disorders other than ADHD.

Typically, the combination of ADHD with other disorders presents more challenges for children, parents, educators, and healthcare providers. Therefore, each child with ADHD must receive a proper medical evaluation by a doctor so that they can determine if the child has other disorders and problems.

So that this does not take you off guard, you must know what I am talking about, because yes, it is true that at this point you feel confused with so much information. The good thing is that here you have an overview of the most common conditions and concerns that can occur with ADHD. Don't sit idly by and urge the doctor if you're concerned about your child's symptoms, which may include:

Problems or Difficulties in Conduct or Behavior

At times, children face situations of discomfort and you can see them angry or challenging before other groups of people or adults, possibly responding aggressively when they are acting under this emotion.

The important thing is that when these behaviors last over time or are severe, they become a worse behavior disorder. Children with ADHD are more likely to be diagnosed with a behavior disorder in the first place, such as oppositional defiant disorder or conduct disorder.

Oppositional Defiant Disorder

When you see kids misbehaving consistently, and that behavior leads to serious problems at home, at school, or with their peers, they may be diagnosed with the oppositional defiant disorder, also known as ODD. This is just one of the most common disorders that occur along with ADHD.

It usually begins to manifest before the age of eight years; however, it can also be seen in adolescents. Children with ODD are also very likely to engage in oppositional or defiant behavior around people they know well, such as members of the family or someone who cares for them on a regular basis.

You should know that children with ODD display these behaviors more often than other children their age. Some behaviors corresponding to TOD include the following:

- Anger frequently.
- Fight with adults or say no to the idea of following the rules or adult requests.
- Feeling like hurting someone they feel has hurt them or caused them trouble; feel resentment frequently.
- Deliberately annoying other people and easily annoyed with others.
- Attributing their own mistakes or misbehavior to other people frequently.

Conduct Disorder

On the other hand, and a very similar one, is conduct disorder (CD), which is diagnosed when children develop a pattern of aggressive behavior towards others and commit serious violations of social rules and norms at home, school, and with their peers.

Normally, these behaviors lead to breaking the law, and those who do not control it end up being imprisoned. If a child has ADHD, they are more likely to be diagnosed with CD.

Children with CD are also more likely to be injured and have difficulty relating well with their peers.

Some behaviors corresponding to CD include the following examples:

- Violating serious rules, such as sneaking out, coming home late at night when told otherwise, or skipping school.
- Behaving aggressively in a way that causes harm, such as whipping, fighting, or being cruel to animals.
- It is also common for them to lie and steal, or damage something that belongs to another person on purpose.

TREATMENT OF HARMFUL BEHAVIORAL DISORDERS

It is important to start treatment early, as it will be more effective if it is adapted to the needs of the child and the family.

The first step in choosing a treatment is to have a full evaluation done by a professional. Some of the signs of behavior problems, like not following the rules, are also signs of ADHD, so it is important to do a careful evaluation to see if the child has both conditions.

For younger children, the highest-ranked treatment is training parents in behavior management. A great ally in these cases is a therapist who helps parents learn effective methods of strengthening the parent-child relationship and responding to the child's behavior.

For school-age children and adolescents, an effective treatment that is used on a daily basis is a combination of training and therapy that includes the child, the family, and the school. Many times the treatment involves the use of medications, but this should only be decided by a doctor.

Learning Disorder

It is common for many children with ADHD to have a learning disorder (LD), so you need to understand that this disorder also brings its own challenges, such as difficulties paying attention, staying focused, or being organized, as well as making it difficult for a child to do well in school.

A learning disorder means that a child has difficulty in one or more areas of learning, but their intelligence is not affected. Learning disorders often lead to:

- **Dyslexia:** It is the difficulty that they present with reading.
- **Dyscalculia:** It is the difficulty that they present with mathematics.
- **Dysgraphia:** It is the difficulty that they present to write.

It can be particularly difficult for a child to succeed in school when they have a combination of problems caused by ADHD and those caused by LD. For this reason, the adequate diagnosis of each disorder is decisive so that the child receives the correct help in each one.

About the Treatment of Learning Disorders

Children with learning disorders commonly demand additional help and instruction, one that is specialized for them. This type of disorder may make the child eligible for special education services at school.

This is a necessary measure since children with ADHD often have difficulties in daily school activities. So the first step is a careful evaluation to see if the problems are also caused by a learning disorder. Schools regularly have their own tests to determine if the child needs intervention. Parents, healthcare providers, and the school can work together to find professional help and treatment that is right for them.

Anxiety

Although you may not believe it, many children have fears and worries. However, by the time a child experiences various fears and worries that interfere with their performance at school, at home, or in recreational activities, this leads to an anxiety disorder.

It is precisely this environment that makes children with ADHD more likely to have an anxiety disorder than those who do not.

Some behaviors corresponding to anxiety disorders are as follows:

- **Separation anxiety:** They feel very afraid when they are away from their family.
- **Social anxiety:** They are very afraid of school or other places where they can meet people.
- **General anxiety:** They feel very afraid when they are very worried about the future and about bad things that may happen to them.

Depression

Feeling sad or pessimistic is sometimes part of the life of any child and person. What is of concern is the moment in which you determine that these feelings of sadness and hopelessness are often there, since they can cause problems.

When it comes to children with ADHD, you need to understand as a mother that they are more likely to have childhood depression than children without this condition. They are more likely to feel this way because they cannot control their ADHD symptoms. What is harmful is when these symptoms are mixed with doing well in school or having good relationships with family and friends.

The most common behaviors seen in children who are depressed are:

- Feeling sad or discouraged much of the time.
- Reluctance to do fun things.
- Have difficulty concentrating.
- Feeling useless or worthless.

Kids with ADHD already have trouble concentrating on things that don't interest them much, and depression can only make it hard to focus on things that are normally fun.

Changes in eating or sleeping habits also present as a sign of depression. For children with ADHD who are taking medication, changes in eating and sleeping may present as side effects of the medication rather than signs of depression. It is always advisable in these cases to talk to the doctor if you have concerns.

TREATMENT OF ANXIETY AND DEPRESSION

It is important that if you are going through this situation, you understand that the first step in treatment is to speak with a healthcare provider who will do an evaluation.

Signs of depression, such as having trouble concentrating, are also signs of ADHD, so it's important to do a careful evaluation to see if your child has both conditions.

Another detail to consider is that only a mental health professional is capable of using an effective therapy plan to improve what is happening to the child and the family. Early treatment is timely and includes therapy for the child, counseling for the family, and even a combination of both.

In addition, you have the opportunity to get into therapy programs offered by schools. For children of an early age, it is of great importance that parents accompany the process during treatment.

That is why cognitive behavioral therapy is presented as a form of therapy used to treat anxiety or depression exclusively in older children. It makes it easier for the child to change their negative thoughts for other ways of thinking that are more positive and effective. To a large extent, a consultation with a healthcare provider helps you determine if medications should also be part of the treatment.

Difficult Relationships With Peers

ADHD can make it more difficult to get along with peers or friends. This is why having friends is important for children's well-being and can be beneficial for long-term development.

It is a fact that some children with ADHD have no problem getting along with other children, while others have difficulty relating to others, may not have close friends, or may even be rejected by other children.

The truth is that children who have difficulty making friends are also more likely to develop anxiety, behavioral and mood disorders, use and abuse substances, or engage in criminal behavior in adolescence.

How Does ADHD Interfere With Relationships With Others?

There is no certain diagnosis of how ADHD interferes with social problems, as these inattentive children sometimes appear shy or introverted at the discretion of their friends or peers. Children with symptoms of impulsivity or hyperactivity may be rejected by their peers for being nosy, not being able to wait their turn to speak, or acting aggressively.

Children with ADHD are also more likely than those without ADHD to have more disorders that interfere with good relationships with other people.

Important: Just because a child has ADHD doesn't mean they won't have friends.

For the most part, not all children with ADHD have difficulty getting along with others, because, for children who do have difficulties, many things can be done to help them with their relationships.

You have to keep in mind that the more difficulties a child has with the other children with whom they interact are noticed, the more successful the intervention can be. Although researchers don't have definitive answers about what works best for kids with ADHD, there are some things to watch out for and keep in mind to help your kids build relationships with others.

- This will take a few minutes a day and is to pay attention to how your child gets along with other children. These relationships can be just as important to their performance in school as their grades.
- Talk regularly with people who play an important role in your child's life (this group of people includes teachers, school counselors, extracurricular activity leaders, health care providers, etc.). It is always necessary to keep abreast of the social development of the child in the context of the community and the school.
- Include your child in activities with other children and in this way connect with other parents, sports teachers, and other related adults in your child's life about any progress or problems that may occur with them.

Programs that they participate in with other children can be helpful, especially for older children and adolescents. Programs where other children perform and where they practice getting along with others can be helpful. Commonly schools and communities have this type of program; find out about them. You can contact your doctor and a worker at your child's school to find out about these programs that could be of great help.

Beware of the Risk of Injury

Children and adolescents with ADHD are more vulnerable to more frequent and severe injuries than their peers who do not have ADHD. Research points to the idea that children with ADHD are prone to any of the following things happening to them:

- Getting hurt when walking or bicycling.
- Getting a head injury.
- Hitting more than one part of the body.
- Suffer from accidental poisoning.

The truth is that there is a need for more research to understand why children with ADHD get injured, but inattention and impulsiveness likely put them at risk.

An example of this is that a young child with ADHD may not pay attention to cars while riding a bike or crossing the street, or may do something dangerous without thinking about the possible consequences. Compared to drivers without ADHD, teens with ADHD who drive are more likely to have driving problems, such as breaking traffic rules, receiving tickets, or crashes.

There are several ways to provide care for children to prevent these injuries from occurring and to keep them safe. If you are wondering what you can do in this situation, you can take these steps to protect children with ADHD. However, later in the following chapters, you will have more detailed guidelines about what to do.

SOME GUIDELINES THAT YOU CAN USE FROM NOW ON

- Have your child wear safety gear, such as a helmet, when they ride a bike, skateboard, or skates. Remind kids whenever you can to be careful around cars and teach them how to stay safe on the road.
- Supervise your child when they are participating in activities or in places where they are more likely to get injured, such as when they are climbing or when they are near a pool or in water.
- Keep medicines, tools, and household products away that may present a risk.

The truth is that in the case of children who are eight years old and older, they face additional risks when driving. They must be very careful to avoid distractions, such as driving with others in the car, talking on the cell phone, texting, eating, or playing on the radio. Like all kids.

In the case of those who are already teenagers, parents should talk about driving rules, the importance of complying with them, and what would be the consequences of breaking them. Parents can create management agreements with teens that put these rules in writing to set clear expectations and limits.

Comorbidity

ADHD, as has already been made clear in previous points, is a diverse neurodevelopmental disorder that begins in early childhood, and is caused by the interaction of a biological predisposition with environmental factors, due to a deficit in cognitive self-regulation.

You certainly don't know this at the moment, nor do you know that the symptoms tend to improve with age. However, in a frequent percentage of cases, the symptoms persist into adulthood. It is estimated that in approximately 60% of cases, the symptoms are clinically significant in adulthood.

ADHD is common, and has a variable prevalence according to

studies, ranging from 7–10% in childhood, and 2.5–5.5% in adulthood, and has significant psychosocial adjustment problems.

This is where the term comorbidity comes in, which is defined as the presence of two or more simultaneous nosological conditions, and in ADHD, it can be considered the norm rather than the exception. This implies a worse functioning and prognosis, especially in those cases in which it is multiple.

Various authors define comorbidity as the simultaneous occurrence of two or more unrelated nosological conditions. Although, as scientific advances are taking place, common links have been found, both in the biological bases and in the brain mechanisms involved, both in ADHD and in other associated comorbid disorders, such as ADHD and oppositional defiant disorder (ODD) or autism spectrum disorders (ASD).

According to a study, children diagnosed with ADHD meet other criteria for other psychiatric disorders. On the other hand, it has been found that ADHD associated with comorbidity has more difficulties in psychosocial adaptation.

It is for this reason that, when comorbidity is mentioned, you understand that it represents one of the great challenges in the detection and diagnosis of ADHD.

As I have told you from the beginning, sometimes the symptoms of ADHD are confused with the symptoms of other disorders, such as anxiety, given that anxious people usually show an increase in inattention and even hyperactivity in complex situations.

The important thing here is that you can determine that, on other occasions, ADHD symptoms are modified when there is another comorbid problem. An example is, anxiety-associated ADHD tends to present with less impulsiveness than the non-comorbid group. Comorbidities simply complicate the evaluation.

Fact: About 67% of children with ADHD have at least one psychiatric or neurodevelopmental disorder compared to 11% of children without ADHD. Comorbidity is often multiple, since of these, 33% of ADHD would present a single comorbid disorder, 16% two, and 18% three or more.

In adolescence and adulthood, there are other comorbidities, one of the most prevalent being the abusive use or dependence on toxic substances in 25–50%.

With this information, the idea is that as a parent, you are aware of the scenario that you may face and that you can understand some of the references that a doctor makes to you in consultations. It is common for you to attend a consultation and then leave with all these questions or doubts because it turns out to be a lot of information and I know that it can stress you out because it is about your child.

CHAPTER 3
CAUSES OF ADHD IN CHILDREN

O nce you know the ways to detect if there is a pattern that your child follows and that this is strongly associated with those previously exposed to ADHD, and you come to verify that it is indeed ADHD, it is common that you want to get involved in everything related to it and its causes. Well, you will learn about it in this chapter.

It is possible that after reviewing the symptoms and conditions explained in chapters 1 and 2, you are wondering why this is happening, and why to your child, and with it a series of doubts that you are going to know in this chapter.

Certainly, the origin of ADHD is unknown up to now, as well as the specific factors that contribute to its appearance. Currently and despite the multiple investigations carried out in this field, speaking of a specific cause is not a fact.

Incident Factors in the Development of ADHD

Studies to date affirm that there is no single cause that generates ADHD and the characteristics of its symptom picture. On the contrary, it originates, rather, in response to the interaction of many factors during the gestational stage.

It is starting from this point that it is possible to distinguish be-tween incident factors of biological origin and psychosocial-environmental factors as possible triggering, facilitating, or aggravating agents.

Genetic Factors

The truth is that it has been proven that there are influential elements of hereditary origin that explain the appearance of the disorder in 80% of cases, and there is also the probability of presenting the major disorder if a parent suffers from it, which means that if the father or the mother has ADHD the risk of suffering from the disorder is multiplied by 8.2.

Another important point is that the heritability coefficient of ADHD is 0.76, that is, if the child has ADHD, 76% may be due to a genetic cause. Apart from these numbers, as occurs with other psychiatric disorders such as depression or schizophrenia, there is no direct genetic action that affirms that children will develop it if a parent has ADHD.

On the other hand, there are molecular genetic studies that are associated with the fundamental disorder of various genes on different chromosomes and their copy number variations.

One can speak of a polygenic inheritance disorder, this means that multiple genes contribute to the ADHD phenotype.

Fact: Although it is usually a very rigorous piece of information, it is necessary to take into account that the main candidate would be the DRD4*7 gene, on chromosome 11, which is responsible for producing the D4 receptor for the dopamine neurotransmitter. In the case of those affected by ADHD, this gene is seen to be altered in up to 50–60% of cases.

For this reason, ADHD cannot be seen only as social complexity, or something related only to the child's environment and education, it also originates in large part from specific modifications in certain chromosomes that make up the human genome, as has been discovered to date.

Causes From the Point of View of Genetics

ADHD has been well-defined as a neurodevelopmental disorder resulting from an alteration or variation in the growth and development of the brain and is related to cognitive, neurological, and psychiatric dysfunction.

Certainly, this condition, along with others known as autism spectrum disorders (ASD), specific learning disorders, and tic disorders, among others, are included within neurodevelopmental disorders without a specific cause identified, other than the one discussed above.

The truth is that this could change as the current genetic research that focuses on this group of disorders is increasingly emphatic.

The Perspective of Molecular Genetics as a Cause

Molecular genetics, through a DNA/RNA sequence, greatly facilitates the study of the structure and function of genes. It is estimated that 70% of ADHD is due to genetic factors related to mutations of various genes.

On the other hand, it has been verified that several genes encode molecules with an important role in cerebral neurotransmission and that reflect variations that trigger ADHD.

These genes considered by experts as "defective" will dictate to the brain how to use neurotransmitters such as dopamine (DA) (responsible for inhibiting or modulating neuronal activity involved in emotions and movement). Therefore, it has been concluded that the disorder may be due to a failure in the development of the brain circuits that support inhibition and self-control.

Although this is a deep subject, you should know that the genes associated with the manifestations of ADHD are the genes that code for dopamine transporters and receptors and the norepinephrine transporter gene. It is usually appropriate to investigate and learn about them because maybe you will find many answers.

Despite the significant association with ADHD, the effects are small, so it is likely that the likelihood of developing ADHD depends on several genes, and therefore there may be several different combinations of genes. The truth is that, in these cases, the most consistent finding will be found in the regions of the DRD4 gene, as mentioned above.

It must be taken into account that when a case of ADHD is detected, the siblings, as well as the parents, have a high probability of having or having had ADHD.

Heritability of ADHD

Historically, studies of relatives have indicated that there is a prevalence of ADHD among parents and siblings of patients with ADHD. The risk or probability of ADHD in a child can reach 60–90% if one of the parents suffers from it.

Conversely, a parent or sibling of a child with ADHD has a 2–8 times greater risk of suffering from this same disorder than the general population. Studies have shown a higher incidence of ADHD in biological parents compared to adoptive parents. At the same time, they show that hyperactive children tend to look more like their biological parents than adoptive ones.

Environmental Factors

Another view on ADHD is that it can be acquired or derived from biological factors acquired during the prenatal, perinatal, and postnatal periods. That is to say, it is capable of influencing whether during the pregnancy it was exposed to the consumption of alcohol, nicotine, and certain drugs, or if the baby during prematurity had a low birth weight, as well as brain alterations such as encephalitis or trauma or if it was exposed to high lead levels in early childhood.

This condition has also been associated with food allergies, although more research is needed on this.

Psychosocial factors cannot be left aside, which can influence and modulate the manifestations of ADHD. The severity and expression of symptoms can be affected by the gene-environment interaction.

Neurochemical Factors Perspective

There are also neurochemical theories that describe the origin of the behavioral, cognitive, and emotional dysfunctions typical of ADHD as a failure in the process of development of the cerebral circuits of the prefrontal cortex, the basal ganglia, and the frontostriatal connections. This causes failures in the executive system of the brain and the mechanisms of inhibition and self-control.

These events in brain function occur due to an imbalance in the neurotransmitters dopamine and adrenaline, which causes the production of these two neurotransmitters to be irregular.

It is due to this dopamine and noradrenaline deficit that problems are generated in the regulatory circuits of various areas of the brain such as the prefrontal cortex, the corpus callosum, and the basal ganglia, which alters the functioning of executive functions. They are responsible for directing the focus of attention, planning, organizing, and regulating behavior, and inhibiting irrelevant stimuli from the environment, so you must understand that ADHD originates from these failures.

Psychosocial Factors

Some studies relate some external agents as precipitants or contributors to the appearance of ADHD during the gestational stage or near birth, such as smoking and episodes of maternal stress and anxiety during pregnancy. However, there is no conclusive scientific evidence that there is a cause-effect association between these variables.

It has been determined that a certain parenting style and education are not the origins of the disorder, but it does contribute to aggravating the symptoms and the evolution of the disorders in children who are already diagnosed, so the choice of appropriate psychological, educational, and family interventions is a measure that must be taken immediately because it contributes to an improvement in symptoms and a better prognosis.

Factors That Do Not Cause ADHD

Once all the factors that can cause ADHD have been seen, it can be said that the exact cause is currently unknown, despite the various investigations carried out in this regard.

The truth is that the studies to date propose that there is no single cause that causes ADHD and the characteristics of its symptoms. The theories suggest rather that it is a response to the interaction of many factors during the gestational stage.

Starting from this point, you can already distinguish between factors of biological origin and psychosocial-environmental factors as possible triggering agents, facilitators, or aggravating factors of the situation and get out of your mind theories of guilt or others that I know tend to torment you.

Currently and with the increase in cases of ADHD, many myths have been created regarding the causes and origin of attention deficit disorder and hyperactivity or impulsivity. All fed from the ignorance of the disorder and the lack of accurate information, and who persist in irrational beliefs about possible cause-effect relationships. Do not fall for this!

It is this type of falsehood that generates feelings of guilt in families and educators, and in children, it promotes more problems that contribute to labeling and misunderstanding by others. The idea is to understand and help.

After all that has been explained regarding the causes, it is important that as a parent, you keep in mind that it is necessary to clarify the variables that are not the cause of ADHD, as well as to underline once again the idea that you are not responsible for your child's condition.

For this reason, I present a list of aspects that are not influential in the development of ADHA that you should take into account when explaining this disorder to others, such as relatives, partners, teachers, or siblings of the child with the condition:

- Mother's age at the time she bore the child.
- The factor of the month of birth of the child.
- The intellectual quotient of the parents.

- Overstimulation or lack of stimulation in early childhood.
- Episodes of food allergies or exposure to environmental toxins during childhood.
- Socioeconomic and sociocultural status of the family.
- Living in a large or small area, rural or urban.
- Dysfunctional forms of upbringing; that is, families without or with few resources, unstructured, and absence of a maternal or paternal figure.
- That your child has had bad sleeping habits.
- The arrival of a new brother or sister.
- An experience of separation from the parents, no matter how traumatic the situation.
- Having overprotective parents.
- Modifications in the availability of the parents; that is to say, that the father or the mother keeps working, is unemployed, or works outside the home.
- Changes of school, repetition of course, or changes of teachers.
- The lack of a caregiver or nanny figure in childhood.
- Whether or not to have extra academic support (private teachers).
- Spend time with the grandparents, or care and education is in their hands.
- The lack of rules and limits inside or outside the home.
- Diets rich in sugars, fats, additives, or food colorings.
- Submitting the child to a poor diet with no vitamins, minerals, or food supplements.
- The consumption of television, video games, tablets, and the Internet in large quantities, and high exposure to light visual stimuli.
- The intake of toxic substances such as alcohol, medicines, tobacco, or other types of drugs.
- Diseases or pathologies in childhood.

Once it is clear that these factors mentioned above are not the direct causes of ADHD, those who have the condition must understand that these factors can contribute to the worsening of symptoms, increase comorbidity and associated problems, worsen the prognosis, and thereby further favor maladaptation.

Therefore, it is important that you keep this list in mind as guidelines for what you should avoid when raising a child with ADHA since they are decisive in the course of the symptoms.

Although for the moment there is no single factor that can be identified as the cause of ADHD, they suggest that it is a neuro-biological problem, with a high heritability, and on which genet-ic data is providing more information.

The important thing about all this is that many children and adolescents diagnosed with ADHD can have a good life devel-opment if they receive treatment immediately and before the consequences derived from ADHD appear.

The most common problems associated with ADHD are reflect-ed in the relationship with peers, low self-esteem, ups and downs in behavior, substance use, the tendency to live in marginality, or school failure. This is reflected in early diagnosis, which is es-sential for a favorable evolution to take place and a good prog-nosis for the child's life.

Evolution of ADHD in Adulthood

Although it is not the main topic of this guide, you may certainly be concerned about this stage of your child, because you may not be able to take care of them in the same way as when they were small. For this reason, you should know that this begins in childhood with a good treatment action plan, continues into ad-olescence and, in almost half of the cases, remains in adulthood.

It happens that only 10 or 20% of ADHD cases that are not treated evolve favorably into adulthood. Typically, the three key symp-toms of ADHD, inattention, impulsivity, or hyperactivity, persist, with some variation in their manifestation.

Commonly and in the long term, the lack of attention has ef-fects on the other two and is due to two reasons:

- With age, attention demands grow and inattention becomes more relevant.
- The second issue is that hyperactivity and impulsivity are at-tenuated.

Although I have told you that some symptoms improve over time, you should know that many continue treatment into adulthood. As it is also very common for those who are in adolescence to abandon treatment, even encouraged by their relatives and family doctors as a way of not conditioning it.

The permanence of ADHD symptoms into adulthood, especially if you are no longer receiving treatment, can only lead to a high risk of other problems emerging to further complicate things.

These secondary problems are often reflected in low self-esteem, excessive consumption of alcohol and other substances, conduct disorders, and antisocial personality traits. Another detail is that ADHD manifests itself differently in adulthood than in childhood.

The Transition to Adulthood Can Contribute to Three Situations

1. The improvement of symptoms and their disappearance.
2. The persistence of symptoms intensely.
3. The permanence of residual symptoms, such as lack of impulse control, concentration problems, or poor social functioning.

Regarding the two situations on the list, it is clear what needs to be done. If the symptoms subside, treatment will probably not be necessary; while, if the intense symptoms persist, it will be necessary to continue with the treatment. On the other hand, the most complex situation is the third case: when surplus symptoms persist.

These excess symptoms can deceive you, since they may appear to be harmless, but at the same time, they can cause problems for you. For example, the persistence of concentration problems can lead to imminent failure in life projects such as university and problems in certain jobs.

On the other hand, the lack of impulse control can lead you to develop criminal behavior, starting with the consumption of alcohol or other drugs.

Therefore, it is necessary that in each case, an individual evaluation is made by a specialist and thus agree with the patient on the risks and benefits of the treatment to make a decision in this regard.

It is necessary to take into account that the benefit of treatment not only represents an improvement in the three main symptoms, but also contributes to emotional regulation, anxiety, and self-esteem, and reduces the risk indexes of drug use.

On the Diagnosis of ADHD in Adulthood

Although in the first chapter, we told you that the diagnosis must be made at an early age to improve the symptoms, when it comes to an adult where the condition appears in adulthood, you should know that this may be because the person has been able to adapt their lives to their difficulties in a more or less satisfactory way.

What is recommended in this case is that you consult a specialist when facing a more demanding environment, such as admission to an institute or university, or from the university to the working world and thus the social world.

These people have largely managed to compensate for attention deficits with a high intelligence quotient, which is known as people with ADHD and high abilities.

The other scenario is that of people who were diagnosed with ADHD in adulthood and who previously visited different specialists and were never correctly diagnosed with ADHD.

This is partly because academic performance may have been good and the person was intelligent, and partly because they developed symptoms of other mental disorders that masked the ADHD diagnosis.

This is common in the case of women who have been diagnosed with depression, anxiety, or a personality disorder, and may be because the symptoms of emotional instability, low self-esteem, insomnia, anxiety, and frustration were stronger.

While in the case of men, they are often diagnosed with impulse control disorder, substance use, or dysfunctional personality traits, and symptoms of impulsivity, hyperactivity, inattention, and poor organization have been attributed to substance use itself.

The evolution of the disorder in the diagnosed and treated cases can be good in the sense of controlling the symptoms and achieving an acceptable adaptation to the environment. As you have seen, the symptoms of hyperactivity and impulsivity can be mitigated over time and with the maturity of the individual. Although, the lack of attention usually remains and leads to adaptation difficulties as the environment becomes more demanding.

Factors That Determine a Good Prognosis for ADHD

As in all conditions, in ADHD you must determine the predictor variables of favorable evolution. Therefore, these principles of good ADHD prognosis are:

- Diagnose the problem as soon as possible.
- Treatment begins at the time of diagnosis.
- Persist and maintain the treatment for the necessary time agreed with the treating physician.
- High intelligence and low cognitive involvement, evaluated by a neuropsychologist.
- Development of good family relationships and personal relationships such as friends and partners.
- Enjoy being raised in a structured family environment with parents with developed parenting skills.
- Integration into the practice of some sports.

Factors That Determine a Poor Prognosis for ADHD

On the contrary, there are also poor prognostic factors for ADHD, and they are:

- The intensity of the main symptoms of inattention and hyperactivity.

- Diagnosis of autism spectrum disorder or low IQ during childhood.
- Child development at a low socio-economic level—It is due to less access to aid that they are more exposed to marginal environments.
- The appearance of behavioral disorders or antisocial behaviors.
- Consumption of alcohol or other drugs, which is related to the previous point.
- Lack of good sleep.
- Emotional instability with episodes of frustration and frequent difficulties in emotional regulation.
- Affectation to a great extent of the executive function; that is, of the organization and planning of time and tasks.

The Complications That ADHD Can Have

As many must have informed you or possibly have told you, ADHD is associated with academic failure in a way that is independent of the patient's intelligence. A point of reference is in the United States, where only 5% of people with ADHD finish college compared to 35% of people who do not have the condition.

Concerning job development, people with ADHD are more likely to be fired at one point, something that is related to more job changes and a higher unemployment rate.

Here, a determining factor is possible behavioral changes, potential conflicts with colleagues and superiors, poor performance, making mistakes due to forgetfulness, inadequate concentration, and, in general, poor adaptation.

The truth is that this difficulty in adapting can grow if you are also changing companies, peer groups, and jobs continuously.

 As mentioned at the beginning, people with ADHD have a greater risk of suffering injuries, including domestic or work accidents due to forgetfulness, but also traffic accidents due to excessive speed while driving, or due to the influence of narcotics.

It is common for people with ADHD to manifest the need to

drive fast to keep their attention on the road, something that can only lead to an accident. It is for this reason that they are more likely to receive traffic tickets for speeding and are more likely to have their driving license withdrawn.

What you should know is that ADHDH treatment reduces the chances of committing offenses that can be sentenced, so you should not be alarmed but take care that your child complies with treatment.

Detect ADHD Through Academic Performance

Academic performance is the main reason for consultation that parents express when taking their child to assess a possible ADHD.

Although the results of academic performance are not the most important thing in the life of a child or adolescent, it is true that in some cases it can be the beginning of a torrent of problems.

To diagnose this condition, you should not only look at the grades, if the child begins to fail classes and repeat the year, which will mean a significant change in their life, and with it, their self-esteem may drop, they may suffer ridicule from classmates, they are going to change companions, and their relatives are going to be upset with them.

What you should know is that, if they repeat more than one course, they will find that their classmates are younger and it will be more difficult for them to relate to them and this will inevitably cause a clash, since the lack of relationships leads to isolation or seeking friends outside of school.

You should know that children with ADHD are at three times the risk of expulsions and are at greater risk of being involved in criminal behavior.

Children with ADHD who do not receive treatment are at higher risk compared to children who do. Therefore, it has been confirmed that adequate pharmacological treatment can improve the performance and academic results of children with ADHD.

It is believed that this has a positive effect since it reduces disruptive behaviors and improves hyperactivity. In addition, attention during the teacher's lessons and home study improves, as well as the assessment made by the student's teachers contributes to self-esteem.

You can't rule out ADHD in a person simply because they completed college, especially in highly intelligent people who have been able to offset the consequences of inattention with high intelligence.

CHAPTER 4
THE JOYS OF ADHD

By now it is possible that you are clear about the main symptoms of ADHD and that you have already identified them in your child. Certainly, as I explained to you in the previous chapter, difficulty in focusing and impulsiveness are the most common; however, there is a challenge that many do not usually talk about and that is the difficulty in managing emotions. You should know that your child is not far from this and rather it is an area where you should get involved. For this reason, in this chapter, you will take a journey through the feelings of a child with ADHD.

In the past chapters, you learned how the symptoms and conditions reflect, and the factors that influence the DHD explained in chapters 1, 2, and 3. Well, the time has come to answer your questions about emotions.

To begin with, you should know that people with ADHD experience the same emotions as the rest of the people. Commonly what differentiates them is that they feel these emotions with more intensity, they also last longer and can affect daily life.

People with ADHD:

- Feel overwhelmed by discouragement, frustration, or anger.
- Give up very quickly on whatever they are doing.
- Feel that they should avoid interacting with others.

Children with ADHD usually handle their emotions better as they get older. However, some continue to have difficulties into adulthood. In any case, you can learn to control your emotions at any age.

Those who are involved with children with this condition know the main symptoms of ADHD and also understand the importance of digging into what they feel.

Difficulties establishing control over emotions can manifest in different ways in people with ADHD. Many have a hard time stopping their feelings when they are angry or stressed. Others have a hard time getting going to do something when they are bored.

People with ADHD may also:

- Feel frustration easily due to small annoyances.
- Worry for a long time even about small things.
- Have trouble calming down when they are upset or angry.
- Take offense at the slightest criticism.
- Experience excessive urgency to get something they want at the moment.

Why Do They Feel More Than Other People Who Don't Have ADHD?

Those with ADHD have difficulties with a set of mental skills called: executive function. These skills help keep things in perspective and manage how you respond to situations and feelings. They also involve flexible thinking and impulse control.

The other skill of this executive function is that they are probably too focused on how they are feeling in the moment to take other feelings into account, and this is a common issue as well.

An example of this is that they may feel angry and say something offensive, even though the reality is that they did not intend to hurt anyone. These skills develop over time, and in the case of children with ADHD, they can improve the management of their emotions as they get older. The challenges continue until adulthood, so it is advisable to work on them from now on.

How Important Is It to Work on Emotional Intelligence in ADHD Children?

It is a fact that the difficulty that ADHD children experience in the social area cannot be refuted, especially in relationships with their friends or peers, since they have limited knowledge of themselves and their effects on others.

This lack of ability in the social area of children with ADHD occurs because of how complex it is for them to identify their own emotions and the emotions of others. They tend to have a harder time paying attention to social cues than other children, managing them and anticipating the results of this, and finally facing the consequences that these have on themselves and on others. A context that ends up generating problems of social rejection, forced isolation, and sometimes great loneliness.

All these difficulties end up being correlated with deficits in the development of emotional intelligence, or in its management and regulation of emotion and affection.

It is in the investigations in neuroscience and cognitive psychology where it is pointed out that the emotional quotient is as important as the intellectual quotient and certainly their relationship must be harmonious since it determines the healthy development of the child and their future success.

IQ can contribute only 20% of the determining factors for success, with the remaining 80% depending on another class of factors. This helps all educators to understand the importance of emotional intelligence as a basic requirement for the effective use of IQ, and in turn knowledge and cognitive skills.

It shows the relationship between your feelings and your thinking, which is important since they are closely related to teaching and learning. For this reason, it is imperative to use foster activities to train emotional intelligence.

It is important that once you have been diagnosed with ADHD, the next thing is to start working on your emotions, since from an early age, you find programs aimed at systematically stimulating your emotional intelligence.

You should know that this not only applies to children with the condition, but it is also a recommendation for the general child population as well as for those children who show greater deficiencies in these areas. This is recommended in order to reduce the risks of diminished mental health, school dropout, poor performance, maladjustment, school difficulties of various kinds, the appearance of violent behavior, etc.

Training the way ADHD children handle emotions is vital; they must perform self-knowledge exercises, empathy, emotional self-expression, and self-esteem since this will enhance optimal socio-affective development, which will help them to generate personal self-control strategies to face the dysregulation of emotions that they sometimes suffer.

All of the aforementioned will bring you benefits such as:

- Increase in self-esteem.
- Increased chances of academic success.
- Better family and school climate.
- Positive impact on mental health.
- Better successful social interactions.

Activities to Work on Emotional Intelligence

One of the activities that you as a parent can begin to use and thus work on emotional intelligence in your child with ADHD is based on developing tasks in which children can discover the following objectives for themselves:

- Explore the concept of emotional intelligence.
- Find out about the most basic emotions: joy, sadness, surprise, fear, and anger.
- Emotional expression of these.
- Identify the situations that lead us to feel that way and the behaviors that we carry out.
- Know themselves: self-concept.
- Develop empathy or the ability to put yourself in another's place.

You can use these activities through:

- An emotions billboard where the child places their photo in the emotion they feel every day.
- You can also make use of a presentation on a PC or an over-head projector where you explain the concepts they must learn and the activities they are going to develop.
- Show them a video about emotions in cartoon movie situations, so that the child can begin to identify what basic emotions the main character is having, such as joy, anger, fear, or sadness.
- Subsequently, you will pass them a question sheet that will serve as a guide to see if they have understood and attended to the video.
- You can make use of puppets and theater. Without a doubt, it is an activity that will make them burst with emotion and where they usually express their joy.

You can do this activity like this:

It begins by showing them the panel of emotions, where they can place their photo in the emotion that they think they have as a consequence of the course of their day. This is where you will see the emotion they are experiencing and based on this, you will help them see how that emotion can influence their behavior.

Once you identify their emotion that day, you can masterfully explain what emotional intelligence is, and you will be helping them understand it through their previous ideas and examples from their daily life.

Then show them a video about emotions in cartoon movie situations, and allow the child to identify what basic emotions the main character is having, such as joy, anger, fear, or sadness.

Next, ask them a series of guiding questions that will help them better understand the video watched. With these questions, you can detect the attentional and comprehension capacity that they show, and the capacity that they present when it comes to knowing how to identify the emotion in others.

After identification, they will have to face each emotional state, express when was the last time they felt each emotion and what happened then, and, finally, they will have to relate the emotion they usually feel to different exposed situations.

The final idea is to choose a puppet to represent a scene in which the character has an emotion, and with that, you can determine what your child is feeling. Although it is usually an activity carried out by teachers, you can also use it.

The important thing is that they learn to recognize their emotions, the emotions of others, and how they affect them when it comes to properly relating to others.

With all this, you can promote:

- Conflict resolution.
- Channeling of negative emotions.
- Obtaining greater socio-emotional capacity.
- Greater probability of consciously and autonomously controlling behavior.
- Learning to read and write emotionally is one of the best investments that human beings can make for themselves, their children, and their future.

Low Self-Esteem in Children With ADHD

As is well known, self-esteem is the concept you have of yourself, and it is based on thoughts, feelings, sensations, and experiences throughout life. Self-esteem is the affective evaluation of your self-concept and can be modified by the perception of failure or personal success, conditioning your motivation and effort towards tasks and situations.

The relationship between self-concept and self-esteem plays an important role in people's lives; and is related to the level of personal, professional, and social satisfaction.

Children with ADHD frequently show affectation in their self-esteem as a consequence of receiving negative comments from their families, teachers, and peers. They become unpopular children, have difficulty making or keeping friends, often get into trouble, or do poorly in school.

It is these situations that lead children with ADHD to develop the feeling of failing at everything, of not doing anything well, of being useless, of being "bad," "stupid;" and "lazy," despite trying to do things right and it is something that you must take great care of as a parent.

Children with ADHD often turn out to be less happy than other children their age.

Reasons for Low Self-Esteem in Children With ADHD

Low self-esteem can originate from different reasons:

Their difficulties in controlling their behavior cause them to have problems in their relationships with others (friends, class-mates, siblings, etc.) and therefore, they will feel that their social skills are insufficient.

Children with ADHD generally show poor school performance and compare themselves with their classmates and friends, so they end up thinking that they are worth less than them. They realize that it took them all afternoon to solve a project that their friends did in an hour.

They tend to make more mistakes than the rest and they make an effort to do things well, to please others, but the results are not always satisfactory.

It is because of all these unsuccessful efforts that they feel frus-trated, and on many occasions, they exclaim: "Everything I do goes wrong."

Normally they must face activities that demand more attention or self-control than they have, something that they do not devel-op well and thus increases their feeling of frustration or failure.

Sometimes they behave in a very intelligent and mature way, and at other times they seem younger, which is a challenge for their parents and teachers. This baffles the parents, who often get angry with them and scold them, giving them negative in-formation about their behavior.

If they do some tasks wrong, adults stop giving them responsibilities for fear that they will not fulfill them. This is how the child begins to feel incapable and insecure.

It is important to develop comprehensive therapeutic management strategies that help them develop the self-concept of children with ADHD, helping them to recognize the responsibility for their actions, and favor competitiveness and the image of themselves in front of others.

You must not forget that the concept you have of yourself is formed over the years, in all the stages you go through, and each one brings you different experiences and feelings with which you build your sense of worth and personal competition.

The Relationship Between Emotionality and ADHD

Universally, emotionality is a quality of the emotional or belonging to or relative to emotion. While emotion is the state of complex feelings with psychic and somatic behavioral components, and its external manifestation is affection.

In ADHD there is difficulty managing and solving challenges or problems, so you can consider that there is emotional impulsivity. Existing knowledge about the emotional alterations present in ADHD is still limited, especially in relation to the neuroanatomical correlate.

On the one hand, emotionality is conceptualized and structured in consciousness, regulation, and emotional autonomy. While emotional awareness, on the other hand, involves becoming aware of our own emotions, being able to name them, and understanding the emotions of others. That is, it would answer the questions: what is wrong with me, why is it happening to me, and for what; aspects in which children with ADHD have difficulties.

The complexity of understanding the emotions of others is related to empathy, and empathy, in turn, to social cognition. In the case of children with ADHD, they show difficulties in social cognition, which involves the encoding, representation, and interpretation of social cues, and includes the perception of emotions from facial expression and prosody, the theory of mind, empathy, and humor processing.

Emotional Regulation

Here, emotional regulation is presented as the coordination between emotion, cognition, and behavior. It involves the appropriate emotional expression, the regulation of impulsiveness, tolerance to frustration, perseverance in achieving despite difficulties, and delayed gratification.

In children with ADHD there is a deficit in emotional regulation or, what is the same, a certain lack of proportionality related to the executive dysfunction of children, such as planning or organizing activities. It is this alteration in emotional self-regulation that leads to a disability greater than those attributed to the two traditional dimensions of ADHD.

Developing emotional regulation includes coping skills with

negative emotions through strategies and alternatives that improve their intensity and duration, and the self-generation of positive emotions, related to the voluntary and conscious search for pleasant situations that generate them.

The deficit in coping skills and self-generating positive emotions is closely related to the difficulty of "intervening in the consequences" of children with ADHD. Some behaviors of children with ADHD, such as conflict with their parents and social rejection, denote deficits in emotional self-regulation.

In the world of emotional autonomy are self-esteem or self-concept, self-motivation, positive attitude, and responsibility, which in turn are related to self-management. You should also know that with emotional self-efficacy, which refers to the acceptance and legitimacy of one's own emotions, comes the critical analysis of social norms and resilience to face adverse situations; these three aspects are related to self-assessment.

You may notice that children with ADHD often have difficulties self-managing their emotions and self-assessment.

Quite simply, the alteration in emotionality is related to the poor performance of the main daily activities in children with ADHD. The alteration of executive functions and emotional regulation end up having an impact on personality development.

Temperament and ADHD

This may be a subject that interests you deeply because it is what tends to stand out the most in them, and that is that the current trend is due to the explanation of personality with integrating models of the interaction between biological aspects and the environment.

Character, of low heritability, refers to the cognitive processes that influence your intentions and attitudes and is influenced by environmental factors.

Therefore, the character can be understood as the particular way of responding to stimuli based on the different concepts that people have of themselves.

The character has three dimensions and they are self-direction, cooperation, and self-transcendence.

- Self-direction refers to self-awareness, self-determination, willpower, self-confidence, and self-control.
- Cooperation describes the acceptance and identification with others, the degree of empathy and compassion.
- Self-transcendence is the degree of identification as part of the universe and is related to creativity, imagination, and the subject's ability to accept ambiguity and uncertainty.

Finally, temperament refers to the differences in emotional responses and behavior between individuals when faced with environmental stimuli. It is moderately heritable and is related to emotions and automatic responses to non-influenced experiences, which remain stable throughout life.

Four other dimensions that emerge in this cycle are novelty seeking, harm avoidance, reward dependency, and persistence.

- The search for novelty refers to the tendency to intense excitement in response to new stimuli that leads to exploratory activity and reactions that can become impulsive and extravagant.
- Harm avoidance is based on the tendency to respond intensely to adverse stimuli causing an inhibition of certain behaviors to avoid punishment or new situations and show behaviors of pessimism, tiredness, and shyness.
- Reward dependency is presented as the tendency to maintain the behavior in response to social cues, which makes an individual appear sentimental, sensitive, and sociable.
- Persistence is perseverance despite fatigue. It is the desire for achievement, ambition, and perfectionism.

Research on temperament in children concludes with the idea of a higher heritability than personality in adults. Some studies have shown specific patterns of temperament in ADHD and broader categories of behavior problems.

From a general perspective, conduct disorders have been related to high scores in the lines of novelty seeking and low harm avoidance; internalizing disorders, for their part, with high avoidance of harm; and low self-direction, with any psychopathology.

On the other hand, it has been observed that the combination of a low score in the self-direction dimensions and character co-operation is associated with the risk of presenting a personality disorder.

Taking into account several studies, it has been determined that children with this show a worse self-perception of their own intellectual abilities, in the sports area, physical appearance, and social acceptance with respect to children of the same age.

The Severity of Temperament

ADHD severity, as well as low self-direction, are also associated with a profile of lacking in goal according to child behavior assessment questionnaires. That is, it seems that children diagnosed with ADHD are more impulsive and less persistent in their activities, and ultimately show lower self-esteem and feel less integrated than those without ADHD.

This Is How Emotionality and Temperament Coexist in ADHD

Characteristics of emotion and personality associated with children with ADHD have been identified as risk factors for developing adjustment problems in the school environment or in adulthood.

When talking about a typical temperamental profile of children with ADHD, it stands out for high emotional reactivity and poor self-regulation skills.

The effects of the relationship between emotionality and temperament tend to be direct on the child; on the other hand, indirect on the interaction environment due to a mismatch with environmental and transactional expectations due to its dynamic relationship with other characteristics of the child's environment.

AMONG THE DIRECT EFFECTS

A high reactivity that predisposes to uncontrolled and aggressive responses to frustrations. On the other hand, high behavioral inhibition would be synonymous with social inhibition.

THE INDIRECT EFFECTS INCLUDE

Each child affects the environment in one way or another, triggering reactions from other people. Very reactive and negative children receive punishment as a response, which increases the risk of aggressive behavior. On the other hand, optimistic and curious children facilitate sympathetic responses.

The interaction effects of mismatching with environmental expectations in a hyperactive child will tend more to mismatch.

In the event that it is a more open environment, the adjustment can be directed in a healthier and more creative way. Whether or not there is a concordance between temperamental traits and a good ability to control can counteract and direct the tendency to hyperactivity. In this way, positive humor makes it possible to better manage the tendency to avoidance.

When referring to the transactional effects due to their dynamic and continuous relationship with other characteristics of the minor's environment, these usually identify the state of health, the size, the mental level, the family structure, the characteristics of the immediate environment, the parental and school educational styles, the cultural context, or circumstances of psychosocial stress, such as coping with an illness that the parents have, affective losses, and situations of acute stress.

The consequences of the interaction of emotionality and temperament are based on the idea that you are facing a child who is very reactive to the environment:

- They are very emotionally intense at both poles, with two registers: very happy or very angry, very insistent and insatiable, and the child typically harasses you with questions or jokes without realizing the consequences for the other.
- It is common for the child to have little motivation unless the

stimulus is very intense and very immediate. In just seconds they can act as if nothing happened.

- They fall behind in tasks that require effort and end up giving them up quickly, so they seem very disobedient.
- Demands immediate gratification and has a low tolerance for frustration, with angry reactions.

All this information is important to know from the parent's point of view since it is you who is with them every day and lives under the same roof. No one better than you to make the pertinent changes and turn this panorama around.

CHAPTER 5
MANAGING THE BEHAVIOR OF CHILDREN WITH ADHD

ADHA symptoms can cause difficulties in school performance, work, and interpersonal relationships, and all this derives from their behavior, so it is necessary to know how to manage it in a beneficial way. In this chapter, we give you the guidelines to do it.

After reviewing the emotions in chapter 4 and how they experience them, what it causes in their lives and that of others, the rest is to use techniques that help you as parents and guide you to manage what happens to them.

Starting from the need to manage the behavior of your child with ADHD, you should know that it is estimated that 6.1% of children in the United States have ADHD, and all the theories and studies suggest that children with ADHD have more chances of having other mental health conditions, such as mood disorders, anxiety, and autism spectrum disorders.

It is the common difficulties experienced by children with ADHD, which include behavior problems, attention and concentration problems, learning problems, social and emotional problems, and problems completing tasks and projects that create a dark picture for parents who know about the diagnosis.

It is important to understand the importance of proper management of children's behavior, because by implementing effective behavior management strategies, improvements are evident at home, at school, and in life in general.

Characteristics in Social Development Presented by Children with ADHD

- Annoys other classmates in class.
- Does not meet social norms.
- Has difficulty resolving interpersonal conflicts.
- Failing to wait their turn.
- Don't share their toys.
- Expresses the first thing that comes to mind.
- Develop important emotional outbursts.
- Constantly commands attention in class.

It is all these attitudes that usually lead to rejection by their peers. You must be aware that children with ADHD are potential victims of bullying. Therefore, promoting adequate self-control and improving social skills is a vital objective to preserve personal relationships and give the child greater social competence.

The objective of psychological therapy is not only based on the idea of developing the intellectual and academic areas but also the social and personal part that is important and will serve them for personal development.

In these cases, psychological therapy presents different objectives and integrates different techniques and resources to achieve the integral development of the child in all its facets, and for this reason, it is opportune that parents go to it if they have the opportunity.

What Can You Do to Help Children Improve Their Social Relationships?

- From empathy, love, and understanding, explain to them the models of conduct that are expected of them in each context. You must understand that, although it is obvious to you, perhaps there are codes that the child has not yet learned to decipher, so it is important to explain beforehand what is the appropriate behavior in each place.

- For example, before going to a consultation, you must explain to them that there is a waiting room and how it works, that they must remain seated, not raise their voices so as not to disturb, etc. It is in this way that you anticipate situations, and this will help your child gradually gain self-control.

- You can also teach them basic emotion regulation strategies discussed in the last chapter in a simple way that allows them to use them when they are very upset. One of them can be to teach them to relax through deep breathing. The good thing is that there are many interesting resources for children with ADHD.

- It is positive to start reinforcing empathy and reflective capacity by teaching them when there is a conflict or problem with another child, and that they must be understanding in the face of this, putting themselves in the other's place and thus measuring from their inner self the consequences of their actions.

- Model a positive role model through your own behavior. You can do this by speaking slowly, staying calm, being patient, and so on. Remember that children always learn from adults and you should not forget that you are their main role model to follow. You cannot demand what you are not capable of giving. You must be an example for them, even if it is sometimes a challenge.

- Reinforces, without exaggerating, the positive aspects of their behavior, and when it comes to a bad performance, it is advisable to focus first on the positive of the situation and, later, go to what needs to be improved. Always do it from a positive and constructive attitude, that is oriented to change. Children with ADHD usually have low self-esteem, so it is essential to take maximum care of the messages that are transmitted to them.

- As far as possible, encourage positive, open communication based on acceptance, not criticism, with which you will ensure that the child has the necessary confidence to come to you when they need it and thus respond properly. The greater the confidence, the greater the level of influence in the child's life.

- Employ and help them develop basic social skills such as greeting and saying goodbye, maintaining a coherent conversation, giving and receiving compliments, requesting things with politeness, and knowing how to wait their turn to speak or do things. Remember that any everyday situation presents itself as an opportunity to teach the child the skills naturally and spontaneously.

- Enhances their social skills by carrying out activities in which they interact with other children. These skills require training and have a positive effect by giving the child the opportunity to put them into practice once learned. For this, a good idea is group sports to introduce them to a social dynamic and help them enhance their social skills.
- As is well known, children with ADHD present complexities in areas of their lives, but it is also true that they have great strengths that you must promote and show the world. It is known that they are intense, extroverted, energetic, brave, very funny children, and at the same time with a great sense of humor, so you should start from there.

Management Strategies You Can Start Using to Improve Behavior

At this point, you should know that there are techniques to achieve what was said above, and if you have come this far it is because you are willing to do anything. Let's start with these strategies:

Create a Structured and Predictable Environment

Children with ADHD often benefit from a structured and predictable environment, so you can start by including regular schedules and routines for meals, playtime, and academic activities. Here it is also recommended to establish clear and consistent limits for behavior and activities. It would also be helpful to provide a quiet, distraction-free space for homework and schoolwork.

Make Moderate Use of Rewards and Positive Reinforcement

Your child may have a hard time keeping attention and focus on a task, so encouraging positive behavior and focus is ideal, and you can do this by using positive rewards and reinforcement.

This includes verbal praise, play time, or special privileges like going somewhere special. It is important that you are consistent in the application of rewards and reinforcements so that your child understands the expectations and the relationship between their behavior and their consequences.

Setting Clear Limits and Consequences

It is important to set clear limits and consequences for inappropriate behavior. The limits must be clear and consistent, and the consequences must be proportional to the behavior.

Children must understand the expectations and are allowed to correct their behavior before consequences are implemented. It is also beneficial for both you and the caregivers to remain calm and consistent in setting limits and consequences.

Strategies for Managing the Behavior of a Child with ADHD in the Social Context

Implementing effective strategies that help children learn to interact with others requires discipline and perseverance. These strategies are based on the teaching of social skills and the practice of social situations.

In the case of your child, behavior management is presented as essential to help them function effectively in their daily lives and avoid rejection. With proper management, you can help minimize challenges and maximize your child's potential.

This management of behavior in the social context involves a series of strategies and techniques used to encourage appropriate behavior and discourage inappropriate behavior.

These are techniques that can be effective both at home and in the school setting and can help children develop social, emotional, and academic skills.

The main objective of proper behavior management is based on facilitating the development of self-regulation and self-control skills in children, something that allows them to make conscious decisions about their behavior and thus improve their ability to regulate their emotions. The idea is to encourage appropriate behavior and reduce inappropriate behavior.

Fact: It is important to remember that each child is unique and may respond differently to behavior management strategies. This is influenced by the factors explained in Chapters 2 and 3, especially environmental factors.

Remember this premise: What works for one child may not work for another. For this reason, it is important to try different techniques and strategies to determine which strategy is effective for each child.

Also, it is important to keep in mind that behavior management is not a solution that will make ADHD go away. The techniques and strategies can help minimize the challenges your child faces and will face associated with the disorder. Children with ADHD may still experience some challenges.

Therefore, it is important to work in collaboration with those who are professionally managing the condition and thus develop a comprehensive and personalized treatment plan.

Finally, appropriate behavior management is an essential component of the treatment of ADHD in children. Behavior management techniques and strategies can help minimize challenges and maximize the potential of children with ADHD.

It is important to try and experiment with different techniques and strategies to determine what works best for each child and to work collaboratively with healthcare providers to develop a comprehensive and personalized treatment plan.

Know the Importance of Using Effective Communication

Firstly, and when you already handle a context of what is happening, effective communication is presented as an essential component in the relationship with children with ADHD.

Frequently, children with this disorder may have difficulties in communicating clearly and effectively, a situation that leads them to have problems in their relationships with others and in managing their own behavior.

All those who are watching them, caregivers, and educators must learn to communicate effectively with these children to promote their success and well-being.

Effective Communication Helps Develop Social and Communication Skills

It is normal for your child to have difficulty reading social cues and responding appropriately. Therefore, it is important to work on developing communication and social skills, such as learning to express themselves clearly and concisely, understanding social cues, and responding appropriately.

Caregivers and educators can teach children ways to communicate effectively using skills such as active listening, empathy, and expressing emotions.

Effective Communication Makes Use of Clear and Concrete Language

Surely, your child has difficulty understanding complex or abstract instructions, which can cause confusion and anxiety. For this reason, you must use clear and concrete language to communicate with them. Explain the instructions and expectations in a simple and easily understandable way.

Effective Communication Allows for the Creation of Clear Expectations

Your child often shows difficulty meeting expectations if they are not clear and defined. Therefore, you must set clear and re-alistic expectations for behavior and academic achievement. These expectations must be explained clearly and concisely, and children must be rewarded when they meet them.

Importance of Listening and Validating the Child's Feelings

Children with ADHD may have difficulty expressing their feel-ings and emotions effectively, which can lead to frustration and anxiety. Parents, caregivers, and educators must listen to and value the child's feelings, even when they disagree with them. Children should be encouraged to express their feelings and taught how to do it effectively.

Works to Promote Self-Esteem and Self-Efficacy

Self-esteem is a concept that we already explained to you from the point of view as stated by the experts, but on the other hand, there is self-efficacy, two critical components in the develop-ment of a child with ADHD.

On the one hand, and to remember, self-esteem refers to the general perception that a child has about themselves, while self-efficacy is the belief that a child has about their ability to perform specific tasks.

Caregivers can take steps to build the self-esteem and self-effi-cacy of children with ADHD.

Promotes Identification and Encourages Strengths and Skills

Children with ADHD most likely have a hard time seeing their strengths and abilities because of the challenges they face in everyday life. Therefore, it is important to foster children's strengths and abilities to improve self-esteem and self-efficacy.

It emerges as another strategy in search of improving self-esteem and self-efficacy to identify those strengths and abilities of your child and encourage their development. In this process, it is important to recognize that although children with ADHD struggle in some areas, on the other hand, they have unique abilities and talents that are wonderful when you discover them.

So it helps to make a list of your child's strengths and abilities and start working on them. This can go a long way in boosting their confidence and thereby making them feel more capable of facing challenges.

It is also important to support the child in setting realistic and achievable goals so that they understand what they are capable of. You should know that this will allow the child to set their own realistic goals and work towards their achievement. The result will be an increase in their self-efficacy and self-esteem. Goals must be specific, measurable, achievable, relevant, and limited in time. It is also important to ensure that the child has the necessary skills and resources to achieve their goals and the necessary support and guidance along the way.

Another way to improve self-esteem and self-efficacy is to instill resilience, as children with ADHD will likely face challenges and obstacles in their path, and having this ability to overcome these challenges and bounce back from difficulties is vitally important.

This includes teaching the child coping strategies to deal with stress and frustration to encourage perseverance and persistence, as well as celebrating achievements and small victories along the way.

Finally, you should know that promoting self-esteem and self-efficacy in your child guarantees that they can feel more secure and capable of living the challenges of life. To achieve this, it is important to use the techniques presented above and show support in the establishment of realistic and truly achievable goals.

As a parent, you should know that promoting resilience and recovery capacity will be of great help since you will not always be by their side.

What You Should Know About Treatments and Therapies for ADHD

As I have well explained, this neurobiological disorder affects many children and adolescents throughout the world. There is currently no talk of a cure because the strategies explained above really exist to manage it.

However, it is worth knowing that some treatments and therapies help manage symptoms and improve the child's quality of life. There are different types of treatment available, including behavioral therapy, cognitive behavioral therapy, the medication itself, and complementary and alternative therapies.

Important: When it comes to medicines, none of them are recommended in this book, we only limit ourselves to informing you about their existence. The idea is that you take them into account, but with the precaution that only the treating physician should suggest them.

This delimitation is important since there are many cases of fathers and mothers who medicate their children at the suggestion of third parties and this can be very counterproductive. No matter how desperate you are, do not apply any medication without first consulting a doctor.

Learn About Behavioral Therapy

It is a form of treatment focused on teaching specific skills to manage the child's behavior. This therapy is focused on the present and is based on the idea that behaviors are both learned and unlearned.

Behavioral therapy can be used individually or in a group, as well as being provided by a mental health professional with experience in treating ADHD.

It is during the sessions that techniques such as reward and positive reinforcement can be used to help the child improve their behavior. We talked about that in the previous chapter.

Learn About Cognitive-Behavioral Therapy (CBT)

This is another form of treatment that can be beneficial for children with ADHD. Fundamentally, it focuses on the child's thinking and cognition, and how this influences their behavior.

Through it, your child can learn to identify and change negative and distorted thought patterns that are affecting their problem behavior. It is also presented as a way to help the child develop skills to manage stress and anxiety.

Medications to Treat ADHD Symptoms

You should know that there are stimulant medications, such as methylphenidate (Ritalin) and dextroamphetamine (Adderall), the most commonly prescribed to treat ADHD, but remember that none should be applied without first consulting your doctor.

According to testimonials from parents, these medications can improve attention span and reduce hyperactivity and impulsivity, but in different cases. It is important to keep in mind that medications are not the only solution and that they must be used under the supervision of a doctor.

Learn About Complementary and Alternative Therapies

They are useful for treating the symptoms of ADHD and among them are meditation, occupational therapy, and acupuncture, which are presented as some of the complementary and alternative therapies that greatly help to reduce stress and anxiety, contribute to concentration, and also help improve attention, coordination and finally fine motor skills.

Certainly, these therapies are not supported by science and should not be used as an alternative to conventional treatment. As their name indicates, they are only complementary.

What to Consider When Choosing a Treatment

When it comes to choosing a treatment for your child's ADHD, there are several things to consider. First, you must take into account the severity of their symptoms and the age of the child, as some treatments may not be appropriate for very young children, while others may be more effective for older children.

Never forget to consider asking for your child's opinion, since their comfort with the proposed treatment is important.

Remember that the idea is to make them feel accepted and that they belong to a group since this is a basic need in human beings. Remember that social relationships are one of the most important pillars for personal and emotional development in children. Do not isolate them!

ADHD Myths You Should Know

The idea of this book is that you have the tools, techniques, and knowledge to create the best environment for your child if they have this condition, so you must know the good and the bad.

Among them, are the myths that you can commonly face.

The truth is that the ignorance that still exists about ADHD causes the world to issue opinions about the child's behavior and, finally, ends up blaming the parents.

These myths arise as a defense mechanism in an out-of-control situation. That is why this book seeks to shed light on the false myths about ADHD and facilitate its early detection. These are the myths:

Parents Are to Blame for ADHD and the Diagnosis Is Unreliable

This is common and it is about acceptance. I know that it is not easy to accept being told that your child has a condition and that they will face difficult situations. You should know that its origin is biological, and it has a high percentage of genetic transmission (75%).

These conditions affect the ability of people who suffer from them and the condition has several possibilities:

- Disturbs the activity level due to its hyperactive component.
- Deprives or stops ideas, thoughts, or behavior due to impulsivity.
- Disturbs the attention on the actions due to inattention.

Children with ADHD have serious attention and concentration problems, develop inappropriate activity, and have low impulsivity. You simply need to know that this is not the fault of the parents, who sometimes do not know how to control or treat the child effectively.

Therefore, you should not fall into accepting blame, just as you should not feel guilty for other diseases that they present. In the world, there are associations of parents with children who suffer from ADHD, something that you should try if you find it difficult to understand. Their diagnosis is very reliable.

ADHD Is a New Disease, It Emerged in the US, and It's an Invention

ADHD has been known like this since 1994; however, it is from 1865, the date on which it appears in the story *Der Stuwwelpeter*. Initially, it was called Minimal Brain Dysfunction, and later in 1950, it was called Hyperkinetic Syndrome, and 10 years later Hyperactive Child Syndrome or Hyperkinetic Reaction of Childhood.

Since 1980 it has been called Attention Deficit Disorder (with or without hyperactivity) (ADD with H, ADD without H) and as seen in the previous chapter, there are three subtypes: combined, inattentive, and hyperactive-impulsive. Its frequency is similar throughout the world, ranging between 2 and 6%.

The Symptoms of ADHD Are Not Serious and It Is About the Low Tolerance of the Parents Toward the Child

What I have been repeating to you throughout the chapters is the importance of treating ADHD. Lack of treatment only has a negative effect on the child because it reduces academic performance and leads to school failure due to grade repetition and dropout, among other episodes. Many of those who pass the course have gaps in knowledge that hinder the next level.

The lack of treatment only affects their social and emotional life since they do not have the capacity to solve their relationship problems with their peers due to their impulsiveness.

Normally a child with this condition and without treatment has few friends and short-lived friendships, something that only contributes to repeated failures in school and bad behavior. This situation can lead to episodes of depression. Untreated children with ADHD develop negative behaviors such as disobedience, defiance, and even alcohol and drug abuse.

In the case of children who do not receive the correct treatment, it can only be guaranteed that in the future, their job performance will be very poor. To this, you can add problems such as pregnancies at an early age, a higher rate of substance abuse, less job progression, and less job retention.

ADHD Affects Only Children and Disappears in Adulthood

It is true that some symptoms of hyperactivity reduce over the years, losing intensity in their behaviors, but inattention and, above all, impulsivity persist in adolescents and adults.

Just keep in mind that one-third of children with ADHD will stop having ADHD before adolescence, while one-third will stop having ADHD before adulthood, and the remaining third will continue to have ADHD as adults. But some maintain symptoms that affect them, so ADHD is considered a chronic problem that requires long-term management.

ADHD Only Affects Men and Not Women

The truth here is that ADHD goes more unnoticed in girls because they have less hyperactivity and do not present opposition, that is, they are less negative in behavior and learning. They also suffer less depression, but they suffer more anxiety disorders.

ADHD Should Be Diagnosed and Treated by a Neurologist or Neuro-pediatrician

The important thing here is that you correctly manage your child's ADHD and prevent its complications. A correct and early diagnosis is necessary and mandatory. Parents and the child's school environment are the first to suspect ADHD. An expert and trained pediatrician can make an initial diagnosis and initiate treatment.

You should know that the definitive diagnosis can be made by a child and adolescent psychiatrist, as well as a neuro-pediatrician, psychiatrist, and clinical psychologist. Upon having the diagnosis, a treatment plan is then designed, in which a clinical psychologist, an educator, as well as a support teacher, or other professionals, can participate.

A piece of advice in case you don't have other options is to go to a child and adolescent psychiatrist since they are experts in ADHD and can help the parents and the child.

Drugs Are Dangerous, You Can't Use Medication

The first option is not this and you should understand this by now since ADHD must include preparation for the mother on ADHD and the management of the child's behavior, show support and school adaptation, and yes, a medical treatment with medication that really shows improvements in neurotransmitter deficits in some areas of the brain, something that the specialist is in charge of.

As a parent, you can go a long way in helping your child get better by understanding more about their condition. Also, you should have a doctor who is an expert in children with ADHD, with availability and patience to treat the child.

Parents should also define clear rules with consequences and rewards for some behaviors, collaborate with the child on homework, and they can also improve structure and order at home. Also, they must define stable and predictable routines to organize time, as well as eliminate distractions and finally make changes in the child's behavior by motivating them.

There are several effective medications to treat ADHD that are approved for use and these are stimulants, which act on dopamine, and non-stimulant medications, such as atomoxetine, with an effect primarily on norepinephrine. Your choice must be made individually and under the supervision of a doctor.

There is an initial phase of treatment in which the appropriate dose is sought, then comes a maintenance phase and a refinement phase, with touch-ups and attention to emerging problems or new symptoms.

Psychotherapy Is Better Than Medication

Psychotherapy really has its benefits when it comes to helping the child with ADHD and it consists of training the parents on the symptoms to establish the behavior management of the child.

The truth is that there is no evidence that magical methods, which cost money, are of any use. The best thing in these cases is to be wary of easy remedies that promise permanent, fast, effortless "cure" and with a large initial financial outlay. It also happens with treatments not published in scientific journals, which many tend to use and it is a patented device or medication with a secret component or one that is not clearly known.

Medications Are Drugs and Are Addictive

Certainly, methylphenidate is not addictive. Although chemically it is similar to amphetamine, at normal doses and taken orally it does not produce a euphoric effect.

It really decreases the risk that the child will abuse drugs in the future because it decreases their impulsivity. Although you should know that high doses of methylphenidate could cause a euphoric effect, so in children who abuse drugs or alcohol, it must be closely controlled.

It is in your hands to store and administer the medication. Atomoxetine does not produce any euphoric effect nor does it have a risk of addiction; however, this should be consulted with a doctor.

The Medication Interferes With the Child's Growth

Many fathers and mothers often express concern about whether the medication affects the growth of their children, so you should know that some studies have shown slower growth in the first 3 years of treatment, although the clinical significance of these data is difficult to consider.

The truth is that height and weight should be closely monitored and in the case of children who lose weight or do not gain weight adequately, energy and caloric supplements can be used.

CHAPTER 6
ADVICE FOR PARENTS OF CHILDREN WITH ADHD

This is the part that perhaps you were waiting for. Here the panorama is clearer after knowing what I told you in the first chapters. Quite simply, being a mother or a father is not easy and when you have a child with a condition that you must be aware of, the panorama can be complicated, which is why this chapter contains advice for parents of children with ADHD.

No one is born knowing how to be a father or mother, nor are there universities to learn how to be one. It is easier to be a good parent when the child does not cause major difficulties.

It may be that many parents of "perfect" children continually give advice to parents of "problem" children, probably forgetting that the circumstances surrounding each child are very different.

In the vision of traits and qualities, virtues and defects, each person has their own hallmarks, which can be very positive for some things and negative for others, and in what refers to attention, restlessness, and impulsiveness, for excess or default, present a great variety of combinations.

Among those combinations may be your child, who surely has a hard time maintaining attention or staying calm in social situations that require them to think before acting.

For many, these children tend to be "difficult children" because precisely in the period that is most important, such as education, is when these traits emerge. During the stages of development, which is when they begin to require skills such as patience, thinking or planning skills, or social adaptation, these children or adolescents become more active.

The truth is that sometimes the parents themselves come to wonder if this behavior, difficult for others to understand, is not voluntary, seeking to annoy. And you can be blamed for thinking like this because your patience is at the limit due to your own family, personal, and professional circumstances, and above all, because you don't know.

What You Should Practice

You are continually reminded of how badly your child behaves. Teachers remind you every day how difficult it is to have your child in class and how "bad" they are compared to other children. So the first thing to note here is that as a parent, I know you're trying.

Avoid Blame

You simply cannot feel guilty for what you did not cause yourself or of your own free will. No parent wants their child to be difficult to educate, or that they do not relate well with other people. Neither have you wanted to pass on your less efficient genes to your child nor have you wanted your child to behave in a non-adaptive way at times.

No parent wants to spend time taking their child to therapy (of any kind), or want their child to take medication, just as no parent wants their child to get sick, just as they don't want to get sick themselves... or anyone else to get sick. Therefore, if this is so, why feel guilty and anchor yourself in that negative feeling? Why not replace it with an awareness of responsibility, with "looking ahead," with the aim of being better every day: a better person, a better parent...?

Encourages Positive Thinking

Just as Eastern cultures propose, where mothers can look inside and try to feel better every day, waking up every morning thinking about doing something that allows them to feel better, so should you. In the event that a common source of discomfort is your child's behavior, consider what you can do to help them since it is common that they sometimes cause discomfort to others or seem not to do enough to please them.

It is a fact that you feel responsible for them to adapt as well as possible to the world around them, so it is advisable to transfer this positive thought and give them something every day that makes them feel good, satisfied, capable, that simply makes them want to continue learning and interacting with the world.

Benefits Their Development

Children are those beings that you have brought into the world without their permission and, although in the early stages of their development, you must be very aware of them, especially the most difficult ones, it is true that as they grow, you notice that they are independent people, with their tastes, their defects, their virtues, and their hobbies.

For this reason, the idea of favoring their development is to allow them to grow along the path that arises before them, to allow them to move forward, to be themselves and not a version of what you want or a reflection of what you dreamed they would be, or what is worse, that they become what you wanted to be and could not.

Your child with this condition may not need to be a prestigious professional or an exceptional student, even though this idea makes you feel proud. The recognition, by others, of your child's achievements, should not be your priority. Life can be long and each person can succeed at the least unexpected moment and can fail or cause problems at other times.

The fact that a child was unruly when young does not mean that they will be an unhappy adult, nor does it ensure that they will be a happy adult. The fact that they have been a model child or a brilliant adolescent does not mean that they will be for life.

Certainly, happiness or the ability to feel good will probably depend more on the person's inner balance and their ability to adapt to the environment, regulate their emotions and relate to others. And that is modeled over time, so be patient, that each one follows the particular course of their personal development that they deserve.

Understand What Is Happening to Your Child

As has already been said in other chapters, it is a condition with a biological component, which makes it possible to inherit a certain susceptibility to suffering from it. Understanding this clearly can make it easier for parents to free themselves from the guilt that unfortunately appears in them all too frequently.

The same can be used to understand that the child with ADHD does not behave voluntarily in a maladaptive way, but that it is something typical of the condition. Their attention skills are simply more limited than in other people. You must understand that it is more difficult for them to wait their turn and not rush, that it is more difficult for them to reason, and that it is very difficult for them not to be in continuous movement.

However, despite this biological component, our bodies, and specifically our nervous systems, are tremendously plastic, much more than you might imagine, and if you add flexible and inclusive personalities to that plasticity, you have a lot to do to favor children with ADHD and thus manage to hide these symptoms that are usually so obvious to others, coming to exploit other traits in which they are virtuous such as kindness, sensitivity, passion, creativity, characteristics that will help them find their place in life.

It is by exercising that responsibility for the well-being of your child that if someone suggests that your child is suffering from ADHD, you should pay attention, especially if these comments come from the school, from our closest family, or from our own intuition. You must ask for aid.

Ask for Help When You Need It

To be clear about the reasons why your child may behave worse than most of those around them, it is recommended:

- Discuss with a group of parents, and even with older siblings, partners, or caregivers who spend a lot of time with your child to see what they say.
- Talk to the school teacher or tutor. It is possible that, if it is available at the school or workplace, you will be referred to the psychologist or educational psychologist of the center for a possible pre-evaluation. According to their recommendation, it should be discussed, or request another medical evaluation from the pediatrician.
- Visit the pediatrician to find out their opinion and their evaluation of the case. In appropriate cases, the pediatrician will refer the case to a specialist in child and adolescent psychiatry who will carry out a thorough evaluation. Where there is no specialty in child and adolescent psychiatry, surely there is a traditional way of referring this type of patient to a neuro-pediatrician or another specialist. Some of them have extensive experience in these types of cases. In any case, most places in the United States have one or more teams of specialists and reference adolescents, and there are usually several in the private sphere as well.
- Go on your own initiative to specific resources at the social, educational, family, and even health levels through regulated aid associations. There are some that are more general in scope, but others are more specific to ADHD. There are more and more helpful resources for families with an affected member, but some of them are still unknown to the majority.

Follow the specialist's recommendations regarding treatments and resources. If you do not see that your child is being treated well or you believe that what the specialist offers you does not fit your child's characteristics, do not hesitate to ask for a second opinion. The idea is to obtain a diagnosis that is as correct as possible, but also seek personalized treatment that makes it easier for you to cope with and understand the condition. We're talking about beings that you care about and that, in the case of children, have their whole lives ahead of them. Don't be afraid to question everything either, and if one of several trusted professionals has diagnosed your child with ADHD, even if you don't want to accept that they have a problem, the best way to help them will be to assume it and follow the instructions of the specialists.

Certainly, it is the parents who are primarily responsible for the care of their children, so the more difficult the situation and the more unstructured the family, the more help they will need and it is convenient to be informed of the available resources. Because, no matter how much will you have, many times all the effort may be insufficient to provide the best care for your child.

Seek Support From the School

If you are talking about school-age children or adolescents, it is essential to involve those responsible for the child's education at school in the treatment plan. From there, a lot can be done, given the time that children and adolescents spend at school and the importance of the place where they develop. This will undoubtedly have an impact on their ability to relate, their self-esteem, their ability to overcome, and on their motivation.

If you do not feel understood or well cared for at school, the institution may not be the most suitable and you may have to look for another one that is more suited to what you consider most convenient for your child. Try to choose a school adapted to the needs of your child and their personality with a suitable level for them.

It is convenient to discuss it with the specialist who handles the case. The same applies to the different activities that your child does. Especially with teachers, it is often helpful for the specialist to establish contact with them.

 ## Promotes Communication Between the People Who Are in Charge of Their Care

Multidisciplinary work is essential, that is, between the different people involved in their care. Pediatricians, family doctors, psychiatrists, psychologists, therapists, teachers, caregivers, assistants, and everyone who has contact with the child in question, requires implementing communication.

This communication must regularly be with a flexible and inclusive mentality, with respect for the role of others and always seeking cooperation, avoiding confrontation. And parents, as the main responsible parties, have a lot to say to promote the fluidity of this multiple communication.

Do not fall into prejudice. Most people will have one or another problem in their lives and the best way to avoid stigmatizing your child is to start by talking naturally about what is happening to them. Don't treat him like someone sick! ADHD will not stop them from achieving their dreams. Many illustrious people have been or are hyperactive-inattentive-impulsive, and with the right help and allowing them to develop their abilities, they have managed to excel in multiple fields.

Seek the Help That Best Suits Them and Their Environment

Various things can be done between all those involved, so you must choose those that best suit the person in question and their environment. There are treatments with proven efficacy, which would therefore be the most recommendable, but there are other complementary measures that are essential to promote the development of the child, and even to improve the other treatments they are receiving.

Different psychotherapies and medications can treat ADHD and have proven their effectiveness over time. Each method has its advantages and disadvantages and the choice of one or the other must be made with the help of the specialist, in a consensual manner, between the affected person and their family.

You must keep in mind that a good professional will recommend what they consider best for each patient and it does not always have to be the same for everyone, I have told you this. You must inform the specialist of their peculiarities and their way of thinking but also keep in mind that they are the ones who know the subject and who can best advise you.

Along with treatments of proven efficacy, there are other forms of support that can complement these treatments and encourage your child's personal development, increasing their self-esteem or improving their general health, and that in many cases facilitate the involvement of parents or siblings, who feel identified with some of these approaches.

It is important to mention neurocognitive training to strengthen the intellectual abilities most deteriorated by the disorder and thus try to strengthen the others.

There is also neuro-feedback, which is a technique that electrically stimulates brain areas that are less functionally developed, but this should be recommended by the doctor.

There are also diets that avoid foods that contain artificial colors and preservatives, stimulants such as caffeine, excess sugar, or that prevent nutritional deficiencies.

Do not forget the importance of carrying out physical exercises that favor the integration of the child in a group or that allow to highlight their most favorable individual capacities, as well as relaxation therapies, or also the focus of attention, such as visualization techniques or hypnosis.

Artistic therapies or any other that favors the expression of emotions is important and can help your child to a great extent and promote self-awareness.

All these recommendations can help a lot and even favor the main treatment if they are carried out by professionals who are adequately trained and experienced and who are closely familiar with the possible benefits and risks that these methods can have on your child.

 I will always advise you that in these cases it is advisable to be wary of treatments that promise quick results with little effort, especially if they are particularly expensive.

The best thing is to follow your intuition as a parent and the advice of those who love you and those who know the most. Do not fool yourself or expect magical results. Even if you feel more identified with some methods than with others, remember that you have to adapt to your child's true needs and not so much to your own. If you can combine both, better than better.

Set Rules and Limits for Your Child

The main thing is that parents create a stable, solid, clear, and predictable family environment for their child:

- **Stable:** Compliance or non-compliance with the imposed rules will always have the same consequences for the child.
- **Solid:** The rules do not change from one day to the next.
- **Clear:** The rules must be known and understood by both parties.
- **Predictable:** The rules must be defined before they are broken and not after since inappropriate behavior by your child that is not included in the regulations should not be penalized. However, you must take this into account for the next regulation that you establish.

Give Proper Attention to Your Child

Paying attention to them implies listening to them and speaking to them patiently. Explain to the child what their problem is and the plans to help them overcome it so that they collaborate and understand what is expected of them and why.

Remember That Parents Are Role Models for Their Children

Always keep in mind that parents are role models for their children. Therefore, in front of them, you must always be constant and act responsibly.

Encourage Your Child to Perform Well

In this way, you will help your child to increase their self-confidence and self-esteem. Stimulate them, emphasizing the quality of their executions, however modest they may be.

Accept Your Child and Love Them With Their Condition

Accept them as they are, without forgetting all the potential they have to grow and develop. However, try not to generate inadequate expectations that are beyond their possibilities.

Create Routines That Facilitate Their Activities

Try, as far as possible, a structured situation at home; that is, keep schedules, avoid excessive stimulation, and designate a quiet place to work and play.

Be Assertive in Communication

Uses authority assertively by saying "no" when the child asks or demands unreasonable things and expressing those orders in a clear, precise, and reasoned manner.

Try to Anticipate Any Changes in Their Routines

Notify them in advance of any possible change so that they can adapt to it and not cause discomfort.

Tell Them It's Important to Think Before Reacting

Calmly tell your child about their bad actions, and emphasize the need to think before acting, since otherwise, we make more mistakes.

Teach Them to Identify Their Mistakes and Find a Solution

When errors occur, you should discuss them with the child so that they can generate alternative solutions on their own. Sit down with them and help them review what happened and generate different ways of acting in similar situations that help them avoid making mistakes. Teach them that the problem is not in being wrong or in the error itself, as long as they recognize it and look for how to fix it or learn from it so as not to fall into the same thing again.

Structure Their Day to Day

Having your child with ADHD live in a relatively structured environment will help them organize the activities that need to be done. Otherwise, an unstructured context, where the same activities can change schedules, will be more likely to generate confusion and failures in their execution.

It will be preferable that you always change your clothes, wash your hands, sit down to eat lunch, brush your teeth, and take a nap to do your homework when you get home from school, rather than doing all these habits every day in order. distinct. In the latter case, some elements may be omitted or not performed satisfactorily.

Know How to Give Orders

A habitual comment of the parents of children with ADHD is the little obedience of these towards the norms and instructions provided. One way to increase the chances of success when you want your child to do something is to follow these simple rules:

- Try not to give more than one order at a time, since it is preferable to wait for the completion of a task before presenting a new activity.
- Segment general demands—The indication "Clean your room" can be separated into "Put away your toys/make the bed/put the papers in the trash can."

- Do not give instructions that may be ambiguous.
- Communicate appropriately—"Be good at Grandma's" can mean very different things to a child and an adult (even to different adults). Instead, "Don't touch things on the table/Don't run inside the house/Don't go into grandma's room" are more concrete instructions that are easier to follow.
- Asking your child to repeat the indication given is a way of confirming that they have understood what is expected of them.
- We must avoid abusing "no" as a resource. It is always preferable to formulate statements in a positive rather than a negative way.
- Avoid sentences such as: "Don't touch the television," "Don't turn off the light," and "Don't talk now." Although they are specific, formulated in a segmented manner, and repeated by the child, they may sound very restrictive, especially when they are repeated many times throughout the day. Instead, you can request the same thing, but in a positive way, saying: "I would like you to sit here for a few minutes," "It is preferable to leave the light on," and "Stay in silence for a few minutes."

Explore the Abilities Your Child Possesses and Begin to Promote Them

Encouraging any natural abilities they may have will increase their self-esteem and feelings of efficacy, and help parents focus on the positive aspects of their child.

In the event that your child does not know what activities they like and in which they can have good performance, they can be accompanied in discovering them.

Because people with ADHD often engage in bad behavior, it's all too easy to lose sight of the positive aspects of children and instead focus on their weaknesses. Keeping strengths in mind can cause a substantial change in the way you look at them, and avoid having thoughts of the type, "They like to disobey and make me angry."

When You Use the Reward and Punishment Do It Immediately

It is common for you to try to modify the way your children behave by applying consequences that are temporarily far removed from those appropriate and inappropriate behaviors.

On the one hand, the child may be able to forget or lose sight of what is the consequence of good or bad behavior that awaits them.

They may also get frustrated by how long they have to wait for the prize, even if it's something they want.

Instead of propositions of the future type, it may be more rewarding for the child to apply a reward system for each exam passed, for each subject passed, and finally, the jackpot can be used if all the proposed objectives are met.

In this way, your child will have more immediate and constant access to reinforcers, which will keep them motivated for longer periods of time. And in case of failure in the final goal, they will not have the feeling that nothing has been worth it, since throughout the year, they obtained numerous benefits for their efforts.

It is important that when talking about meeting the proposed objectives, you refer to those objectives that are achievable by them, not those that parents ideally aspire to. The constant and excessive pressure to perform more than one can only end up producing the opposite results to those expected. An additional consequence is that it produces stress and frustration not only for parents but also for their children. This directly relates to the next point.

Focus on Your Child's Learning and Not on Their Grades

Many people grow up with the conviction that the school grade reflects what they have learned and that, if this is not the case, it is in any case what matters about going to school, since it is objectively reflected in documents and certificates.

In the case of a child with ADHD, the pressure imposed to get good grades can be excessive, making them frustrated and not only not getting the expected results, but also not learning and even repeating the course.

An adjustment in the expectations that you have about the academic journey will most likely end up causing a decrease in the frustration felt by both children and their parents and will enhance school learning.

Avoid Criticism of Their Actions or Way of Being

It is vitally important to everyone involved. Keep in mind that, on the one hand, the child who is described as lazy, fickle, or bad, among other qualifiers, is permanently registering that significant adults observe that in them, and in a great and bad way it will affect their self-esteem and their subsequent behavior.

As for you as a mother, by labeling your child in this way, in general, you leave them predisposed to pay attention to those behaviors that are in accordance with said perception, which influences the good relationship in the medium and long term.

Instead of making statements about whether they are lazy because they didn't pick up their toys off the floor, it's better to point out the request again, omitting all sorts of personal appreciation. If observations are necessary, let them know about the behaviors rather than who is doing them.

Anticipate Potential Conflict Situations

If you already know that certain moments often produce bad behaviors on the part of your child, anticipating these situations, as well as what is expected from them, increases the chances of avoiding these bad moments.

Faced with the repeated situation of running in the supermarket and touching the products that are displayed, even before leaving your house you can comment in a very specific and clear way what specific behaviors you expect from them in a certain place.

Don't Tackle All the Problems at Once

Starting from the fact that it is preferable that there are clear guidelines, requested sequentially and not at the same time, and from the preference of structure over chaos, asking your child to remain still, quiet, that if they are going to speak, not to say bad words, that pay attention to what the rest says, permanently, and that maintain, for example, a certain body posture, will be impossible to sustain.

It is advisable to be attentive to all the problems that a person presents in each given situation, and in front of them establish which are the priorities to attend to and which are not.

It is necessary to keep this series of elements in mind when making these decisions, such as the severity that it presents or the impossibility that it will bring to your child in acquiring new skills, among others; but always without losing sight of the fact that it is not possible to face all problematic situations at the same time.

Do Not Trust a Professional Who Does Not Offer An Accurate Diagnosis

Do not place your trust, no matter how desperate you are, in professionals who use non-specific diagnoses or who do not follow current conventions and rules, and who also use terms such as emotional blockage, immaturity, or laterality problems when it comes to talking about your child.

A good professional must in turn provide the advice and psychoeducation necessary for effective treatment. The functioning of the methods is noticeably affected by the context. For example, a therapist who only works with the child and does not suggest guidelines to parents and teachers to use in situations in which the child develops only decreases their therapeutic efficiency. They also put a weight on the child that they probably can't bear, leaving it to them to be solely responsible for changing their behavior.

Don't Forget About Yourself as a Person

It's not about being a slave. A child with ADHD can cause stress and impact yourself and your relationships, such as your relationship with your partner, your other children, or your friends. Don't let this pass you by.

Take the necessary or required time to perform pleasant activities, allowing you to regain strength to continue your work as a parent later. The same applies to relationships that tend to take a backseat. It will be necessary to look for moments in which they can be cultivated, without the focus of attention being your child.

Remember that in addition to being a mother, you are a person who surely needs other types of activities for your well-being.

CHAPTER 7

STRATEGIES FOR HELPING CHILDREN WITH ADHD IN SCHOOL

It is a fact, and I have been telling you throughout the last six chapters that children with ADHD often have learning difficulties, and in many cases, they can also have behavior problems in the classroom, especially when the disorder occurs with impulsivity or hyperactivity. For this reason, it is necessary that you have at hand the strategies to help them. You will learn about them in this chapter.

You should know that on many occasions, teachers do not know how to handle or respond to the behaviors that the child may be displaying and there may be a risk of labeling these children as rude, disobedient, or disruptive. Therefore, it is necessary to know what to do in this situation.

In the last chapter, I covered ways to shield yourself as a parent and as a person. Now it is time for your child to face a context that you cannot avoid them, and it is that of coexistence in the classroom.

How to Deal With Children With ADHD in the Classroom

Within the ADHD picture, a distinction is made between children who are predominantly inattentive and those who are predominantly impulsive and hyperactive. Some of the traits that you can observe in the classroom in these children are:

- They are usually disorganized in notebooks and homework.
- Frequently they lose or do not bring necessary materials to class.
- They don't finish their homework.
- Frequently interrupt in class.
- They are restless and get up for no apparent reason.
- They have difficulties accepting and abiding by the rules.
- They are easily confused and do not pay attention. It seems they won't listen.

It is important to keep in mind that the child is not always aware of these behaviors and therefore it is essential not to penalize them for it. On the contrary, it is about helping them and teaching them to become aware of their behavior so that they can correct it.

The educational response they should receive in their classroom will be essential to improve the behavior of children with ADHD, and at this point, it will be important to know the nature of the disorder and the problematic behavior in the classroom.

Once you know your child's diagnosis, you must notify the school so that the institution can respond to you and they can create a plan in the classroom according to the needs of your child, understanding that if they interrupt, mislead, or "bother" them, it is not voluntary or premeditated.

You must make teachers understand that ADHD is a disorder that affects attention and executive functions, which are the mental capacities that allow the person to control their own behavior, anticipate the possible future, and, at the same time, prepare and direct their conduct toward the accomplishment of their plan or task.

Therefore, these children find it difficult to regulate their behavior and anticipate the consequences, that is, they act and then think.

That is why it gives the feeling that they do not respect the rules or the limits within the classroom and you must anticipate this scenario. And one of the things that most concern teachers are precisely that: compliance with the rules and discipline in the classroom.

It is important to agree with the teachers to know how to handle situations in the classroom. We need to understand that the teacher must help them with something that they cannot do on their own. Just like they help them solve math problems, they should help them regulate.

Some guidelines that it is suggested to transmit to teachers and thus help the child with ADHD are:

Try to Place Them Near the Teacher's Table

Place them near the teacher's desk so they can have better control of the student. In this way, they can speak to them directly and capture their attention more easily.

The Teacher Should Make It Clear What Is Expected of Them.

Just as it happens at home with the parents, the teacher or professor must also establish rules and the consequences when they are violated.

A sheet with two or three objectives to be met in the classroom can be put on the table (I ask permission to get up, I raise my hand to speak, etc.). This must be visible so that the child can refer to it to remind themselves what to do.

Use Direct and Personal Communication

You can establish with them a signal that indicates to the child that something is not right. For example, approach and touch their shoulder, and use colored cards to indicate how the behavior is.

Use Positive Evaluations

Evaluating the child positively and avoiding excessive or uninstructive punishment that does not help the child to learn about their behavior is a way of coexisting with them in the classroom.

Assign Special Duties

Since the child with ADHD is more impulsive and find it difficult to sit still, it is advisable to give them "missions" that involve moving and taking responsibility for something, such as assigning them to be the person in charge of distributing notebooks, sharpening pencils, going to run an errand, etc.

This way they can be active and you send them the message that you count on them and that you trust that they can do it.

On the other hand, these are other guidelines that you should always avoid:

 PUT NEGATIVE COMMENTS ON THE NOTEBOOK

Comments like: "They don't pay attention in class" is obvious and do not serve to improve their behavior. In any case, it serves to make them feel bad and be scolded when they get home. It is better to describe that in mathematics, they have managed to finish the homework or have helped a classmate.

PUNISH NEGATIVE BEHAVIORS

It is necessary to establish consequences for those behaviors that are really serious and try to redirect those that are inherent to the disorder.

Mention Only What Is Wrong

It is untimely and a mistake not to reinforce what the child does well because even if you think that what they have to do is be attentive and quiet in class, it is something that the child with ADHD finds very difficult.

Generally speaking, working with a child with ADHD in the classroom requires knowing the disorder and being sensitive to it. Therefore, you need to sit down with the teachers and explain the situation, have effective communication about what can be done with them, and understand that the child does not do things for the sake of it, but for an underlying cause that the child cannot control without training.

It is vital not only the detection and diagnosis, but the joint work that parents, teachers, and specialists do with the child. Communication with the specialist who works with the child individually is necessary, both with the specialists and guidance departments, since they can provide effective tools and strategies to work with these students in the classroom.

In order to intervene adequately, all the people involved in the education of the child must act in a combined and cooperative way. At this point, some techniques are presented to intervene in the classroom that can be of great help:

- Don't pretend that the teacher is an expert on ADHD; there are experts who can help you.
- Ask the child how you can help them. Understanding how they are is the first step to understanding how we can act.
- Urge the teacher to create a good climate and atmosphere in the classroom. They must feel comfortable in the space they learn.
- Have them write the rules. Children with ADHD build trust as they know what is expected of them.
- The teacher must repeat and write the rules or instructions. Children with ADHD need to hear things more than once to understand them.
- That the child has permission to ask questions and that the teacher uses glances that involve them, glances that help to regain their attention.
- Sit the child close to you; this will help them not to be constantly distracted.
- Avoid punishments; it will not serve to improve their attention or interest in what they learn.
- Make a calendar to organize all the activities you have planned.
- Help children to make their own calendars.
- Avoid timed evaluations.
- Provide times for the child to leave class.
- Frequently monitor the progress of their activities.
- Change long activities to several short activities.

- Introduce educational innovations whenever you can.
- Do not overstimulate the child; anticipate situations.
- Issue praise and awards to children. Emphasize success whenever possible.
- Teach them to outline and underline; it is important that they learn to structure themselves.
- Use feedback to help them become self-observers.
- Make learning a game.
- Responsibilities are important within your possibilities.
- Try to have a Home-School-Home communication note-book.
- Make daily progress reports.
- Have them write notes to themselves so they remember their questions.
- It is important that, in the projects, each child has a partner.
- Hold meetings with parents often. Avoid only meeting for problems or crises.
- Repeat things as many times as necessary.
- Propose energetic and fun activities.
- Find their moments of brilliance.
- Ignore unwanted behaviors and apply reinforcement to those you consider appropriate.

URGE THE TUTOR OR TEACHER TO KNOW THE SITUATION OF YOUR CHILD

It is recommended and necessary that the teacher is informed about students who show difficulties.

Through meetings with the family, the teacher should be aware of the child's functioning, needs, and weak points, as well as the way to help them.

They should not hesitate in the diagnosis. Urge them to assume their role within the process and facilitate their help to the different agents to achieve the objectives.

It is important that the teacher is aware of whether the student is following any treatment, and whether there are specific medical indications.

Deepen the Knowledge About the Condition

From the position of teacher or tutor, it is essential to assume the responsibility of being an educator of a student with difficulties. The teacher must be aware that their role in the classroom directly influences not only the student's learning but also their emotional state, as well as their evolution and positive development. For this reason, they must have basic knowledge of how to act with a student with ADHD.

Although it is something that escapes the hands of parents, it is good to encourage them to take courses, do self-taught training, promote courses for the teaching staff of the center, read and research on the subject, and go to the guidance service for advice are some of the guidelines to be followed by a teacher who wants to give a good educational response to students with ADHD.

Promote the Bond Between Teacher and Student

Establish a positive relationship between student and teacher. More than any other child, students with ADHD need positive support, praise, and encouragement.

It is recommended that the teacher show interest when the student is working at their desk. Approaching their table regularly and asking them if they have any questions or need support is a way of giving the student security and encouraging them to continue working.

It's also important not to draw their attention in public. It is better to choose to communicate discreetly, without the rest of the group finding out. With a snap of your fingers or by placing your hand on their shoulder, you can bring them back to your attention. It is important that the teacher agrees with the student on some signals that make them understand that they must correct something or continue with their work.

WORK ON SELF-ESTEEM

Accept difficulties. Treat difficulties normally without giving them excessive importance, both for the student and for the group. Publicly remind that no one is perfect and that everyone has their rhythm.

Identify efforts. Remind the student, both privately and publicly, that their intervention has been very good, that their collaboration has been very positive for the result, that the effort is notable and visible, that the change in attitude and behavior is something that everyone is interested in evaluating very positively, etc.

Try to change the language. Try to express yourself more positively by avoiding expressions like, "Okay, but you can do better." It is preferable to use expressions like: "Very good. Next time try to improve this." Change negative messages for messages of encouragement for the future.

FOSTER INTEGRATION

The teacher should promote activities and tasks where the student with ADHD can stand out positively in the eyes of the group (highlight their skills).

In addition, they must promote inclusion within the group with activities and group dynamics, giving them an important role within it. Thus, the student integrated into the group will collaborate to achieve joint objectives, sharing the success of the result with their classmates.

VIEW DIFFICULTIES NORMALLY

Promote reading aloud even if they have reading difficulties and make mistakes, it should be something that everyone should see normally. You have to give them time to be able to rectify and repeat, without pressing or instilling fear of error. Not only students with ADHD have reading difficulties, so reading aloud will help destigmatize that only the student with ADHD has difficulties.

THE TEACHER MUST BE ADAPTED TO THEIR NEEDS

The child should sit in a place where the teacher can supervise them without having to get up, also be away from distractions (windows, noise, door...), and be close to classmates who help them copy or complete the notes and tasks.

Instructions should be given with physical proximity and eye contact, one at a time, in a concise, clear manner, and always making sure to ask for feedback (make sure they understand by asking them to repeat it).

If the teacher identifies that the student needs measures that go beyond their competence in the classroom, they must inform the counselor to draw up a more specific plan.

CHAPTER 8

LIVING WITH A CHILD WITH ADHD: EXPERIENCES OF OTHER PARENTS

The fear that their child will suffer or have difficulties is an idea that parents cannot help but feel. We often run into various kinds of challenges throughout our lives, which is why in this chapter we will talk a little about diagnosing attention deficit hyperactivity disorder (ADHD) in our children.

It is normal to ask a lot of questions and not have answers for all of them. ADHD affects attention, self-control, and the ability to learn in children. Its symptoms can vary in severity and type, but generally include trouble concentrating, hyperactivity, and impulsive behaviors.

The thought that our little ones may have difficulty concentrating, learning, and socializing with their peers can be distressing. Feelings of guilt can arise and emotional support is essential to help us cope with the situation.

The good news is that today we have the voices of thousands upon thousands of parents who have found effective ways to help their children thrive. These experiences can be a valuable source of support and guidance. By talking with others who have been through similar situations, we can find new perspectives and tools to handle difficulties that may arise.

Our goal is to gather experiences from other parents living with a child with ADHD and offer support and guidance to those who may also be experiencing this situation.

You'll find stories, tips, and strategies to help children cope with their condition. Topics such as the treatment of ADHD, how to talk to children about their diagnosis, how to deal with impulsive behavior, and how to manage school and home will be discussed.

The Family Context and Its Influence on ADHD

As we have already said, this condition is the result of the interaction of environmental risk factors and the susceptibility of multiple genes. We tend to overlook the real influence of the psychosocial environment as a modulating factor in the symptoms and most of them are understood and managed by the family, school, and society.

Of course, never trust all the information you find. Having a child diagnosed with ADHD is not a tragedy and it is always up to us to determine and direct a positive impact on both our children and our lives.

The intervention directed at the child offers a beneficial experience for the whole family. The vision that parents have of their child is more positive and relationships in the family system are strengthened.

The intervention aimed at families reduces the level of stress in parents, which allows them to use more effective educational guidelines that have a positive result on the child's behavior; that is, parents and children influence each other.

It is necessary that counseling programs for parents and family members take into account the impact generated by the diagnosis in the family system and be instructed in strategies for stress management, working specifically on their emotions, the perception or negative attributions they have of the child and how they can build an educational style based on effective and balanced communication for all involved. You also have to learn and put into practice behavior modification techniques, when and how to use them appropriately, and how they can cause parents to increase confidence in themselves and their children.

The family has a clear modulating effect on the evolution of attention deficit hyperactivity disorder. These treatments have a positive effect on the family, reducing stress levels, feelings, and attitudes of parents and improving the behavior of children.

What Should We Do as a Family and What Not?

It is important to keep in mind that children with ADHD are more easily frustrated, explosive, and upset. Especially in ambiguous, repetitive, monotonous, and not very stimulating situations. They need to be accompanied and given solutions. Therefore, we recommend that parents:

- Create a routine. Children should be busy during the day and, if possible, make it resemble the routine of school weeks. Establish a schedule of daily habits. It must include the schedule of the habit of sleep, breakfast time, and what we will have for lunch and dinner. It is important that they dress and maintain a daily hygiene routine also.
- That the planning is in writing. It must be visual and with different colors to delimit the weeks.
- The children must participate in the planning and make sure that they agree with it, that it is realistic for everyone, and that they understand it.
- Always do homework in the morning, after breakfast.
- The time for games, leisure, crafts, sports, music, and more is recommended to be left for the afternoons. It is also advisable to put in which cases will be done with the parents and which will not.
- Establish the schedule and time limit for the use of electronic devices. You should not worry; its use can also be beneficial if they are used for educational purposes.
- As far as possible, the child should have conversations on the phone or by video call with their friends.
- They must carry out extracurricular activities that can be accessed in person or with virtual classes.
- Lower the level of demand that is transmitted to them.
- Make use of motivation and positive reinforcement as the

main tool. You can use small prizes and points that can be exchanged for some candy or a few more minutes with the tablet and thus stimulate responsibility and value for themselves.

- Avoid as much as possible direct confrontation, threats, and punishment.
- Explain what is expected of them, but also what they can expect from us.
- Hold conversations about emotions and feelings and not just about orders, schedules, and duties.

Cases of Parents With Children With ADHD

We must highlight the influence of parents using educational guidelines based on respect, affection, firmness, effective communication, and knowing how to control their emotions during the evolution of symptoms.

The purpose of telling you these stories is to understand that sometimes the secret lies in prioritizing our children's feelings and helping them walk their path, the one they need, overcoming the obstacles of each day.

With love and patience, children can acquire a series of guidelines and tools that make it possible for them to lead a full life like any child their age, and that in the future they will be full and self-sufficient adults.

How the Right Treatment Can Change a Mother's Life

Since childhood, the character of her little one generated many difficulties. He was never still, she asked him not to touch something and he did exactly the opposite. This caused him to suffer many accidents: he fell often, broke his leg, had stitches placed in his chin, almost drowned in a swimming pool for diving, and at school, he was always grounded for doing something or hurting some other boy.

His mother tried to set limits, but the behavior was such that it generated a high degree of anxiety in everyone in the house.

Fernando was capricious and constantly had tantrums, when everything went wrong he was violent and aggressive.

This led to the fact that at the age of five, he was referred at school to a center specializing in children with ADHD and there he was diagnosed with ADHD with hyperactivity and impulsivity.

His mother says that everything changed when she began to replace authority with patience and she understood the problem. She discovered that her son really is a sweet, affectionate, sensitive, and good child.

Avoiding punishment, talking to him, and applying a series of simple tools made his reactions less violent and even allowed him to internalize what was happening to him and handle it appropriately. In just a couple of years, the child is better than ever, everyone in the family enjoys him, and he shares and interacts with everyone.

A Couple Tells Us How They Managed to Get the Whole Family Involved

This story is told by a couple who can be considered "normal," with jobs and professions within the parameters considered normal. They have three wonderful children and the middle one is diagnosed with ADHD.

Since this little boy began to walk, he did not stop, and by not finding the right professionals, they spent some very difficult years. They say that at school he had many problems due to his impulsiveness and impatience. It was in elementary school that the teachers referred them to a center to proceed with a possible diagnosis of a possible ADHD, until, after interviewing different experts, this diagnosis was confirmed.

Thus, they began to go to the consultation looking for the necessary psychological support to manage the stress and pressure on them and, above all, work with their son.

Today at school they are happy with him and they are calmer. They affirm that it has helped them a lot that everyone has been involved in the family environment, including their sisters. They all handle tools, which allows them to help him. They see a bright future for their son and everyone in the family nucleus.

Provide the Right Support at the Right Time

This couple realized something was different when their son turned three. The reason: he had a significant language delay. This led them to a path full of consultations with ENTs, speech therapists, pediatricians, and a host of specialists who could not hit the nail on the head. They diagnosed him with a "maturity and language delay," and already in elementary school he was diagnosed with ADHD with language delay.

Parents state that they constantly evaluate themselves as parents and how critical they are of themselves. But, on the other hand, also how they reinvent themselves day by day to achieve new goals, the patience they put into practicing daily, and the tools they use with their son.

Time has made them radically change their initial perspective and they live the condition of their little one differently. They understand that it is a career in which goals are gradually achieved and although there are no infallible formulas, daily work helps to overcome difficulties. They feel like parents of a beautiful child who makes them very happy.

Why Are Comparisons Prohibited?

This couple's experience began when their six-year-old son was diagnosed with ADHD. The first year was an arduous process in which it was necessary to constantly go to the consultation and, in it, they have learned not to compare their children with the children around them. They have understood that he is unique and wonderful.

And although the experience has been hard, with help and patience they are learning every day to overcome obstacles and uncertainties. They now enjoy their child and have understood how he feels and how to use all possible tools to help him.

What We Should Know About Raising a Child With ADHD

We know that raising a child diagnosed with ADHD can present many unique challenges, but you should also know that there are many things parents can do to help their children cope and succeed.

The most important thing we can do to help them is to seek appropriate treatment. This may include medication prescribed by specialists, behavioral therapy, and educational support. It's important to work closely with medical and educational professionals to find the right treatment and follow instructions carefully to make sure everything goes well.

Children with ADHD may have a hard time staying organized

and maintaining structure in their lives. When we establish clear and predictable routines, we can help children stay focused and motivated.

ADHD can affect the entire family and can be stressful and exhausting for parents and the whole family. Hence the importance of taking care of ourselves and finding the emotional support we need in times of greatest need.

A few things you should never forget about these kids:

It's Not Their Fault They Act a Certain Way

Remember that the child's brain works differently; it is a neurological issue. They are not doing these things on purpose, and if they could control themselves and focus more, they would because it is not nice for them to have these difficulties and the public embarrassment that the weight of prejudice can bring.

It's Also Not the Parents' Fault That They Act a Certain Way

We are all human beings and we have defects, but ultimately the way we raise them is not the cause of their inconveniences. Parents correct, and when our children misbehave there are consequences. You also have to understand that what works with other children often does not work with children with ADHD.

Dealing With ADHD Is a Complicated Task

It's not just about being hyperactive or not listening. Children with ADHD face dozens of challenges in their daily life that others, not even their own parents, are sometimes aware of; even the simplest ones that we can take for granted can represent enormous difficulty, and yelling, scolding, and punishment will not change them.

It Is Not Rudeness or a Premeditated Tantrum

Your child may have their rebellious periods, just like everyone else, but when they are already diagnosed with ADHD, behavior that others might consider disrespectful isn't really.

Once the child realizes that they have been hurtful or made others unhappy, they feel very bad; it is not their intention, and rejection can wreak havoc with their self-esteem.

Everyone Does Their Best to Be Happy

The routine of a family where one of the children is diagnosed with ADHD is often full of schedules and checklists to try to keep things in order. They role-play to practice ways to handle situations differently.

This means that children struggle every day to keep things under control at school, although sometimes they get out of control and that's okay.

You Have to Carefully Analyze Whether to Use Medications for ADHD

It's not easy for a million reasons. Children do not usually receive medical routines very well and almost always refuse to take any medication, even worse if it is pills. They cry because they suffer the effects of them and they do not know what is happening to them for sure nor do they feel able to express it. Remember that it is not an option for everyone, but each family makes the decision they consider appropriate and it is not something that is resolved lightly.

Your Child Is Much More Than Their ADHD

When encountering challenges on our way, we tend to focus on the negative effect, and, many times, this is the guiding thread of our relationship with our children. That's why this is perhaps the most important piece of advice you'll ever receive: focus on seeing beyond your challenges and recognize the person who is there, funny, intelligent, loyal and upbeat.

See the beautiful emotions that your child offers you and this will give you a very different perspective on everything, even the smallest thing in your life can have a positive effect on theirs.

CHAPTER 9

ADHD IN CHILDREN: MEDICAL TREATMENTS AND NON-DRUG THERAPIES

ADHD is one of the most common neurodevelopmental conditions in neuropediatrics, child psychiatry, and psychology clinics, and with it, controversy has increased over the various treatments, many of which include the use of drugs and are not well received in all spaces. For parents, this only further widens a sea of uncertainty and doubt.

The differences have almost succeeded in generating a public crusade over the management of ADHD. The reality is that each patient and their problems are unique and doctors know that certainties do not exist; they have to learn to manage and seek answers to all doubts without being an obstacle for the patient to receive the best possible response.

Although treatment remains a controversial topic and we absolutely do not recommend any form of self-medication or non-diagnostic treatment, in this chapter we will review the key treatments you should know about, focusing on those that do not require the use of drugs and that you can implement in your routine in a practical and healthy way.

Of course, we must not fall into the error of thinking that we can solve everything by ourselves. The most responsible thing we can do as parents is direct our little ones and, with the help of professionals, make the most of it and be as happy as we can as a family.

Appropriate Management of ADHD

ADHD can have serious life consequences if it is not detected and treated early. It hinders academic and personal performance and affects job opportunities and social relationships. Undiagnosed and untreated adults have more accidents and a higher risk of addictions and criminality.

Therefore, the main thing is to make a good diagnosis before starting treatment. The presence of other problems that can be confused with ADHD or even accompany it, such as insomnia of different causes, emotional disturbances, autism spectrum disorders, epilepsy, tics, and the like, must be detected and treated.

The causes of this disorder are unknown. Like other neurodevelopmental disorders, it is most likely that the interaction of genetic and environmental factors gives rise to alterations in the formation of brain circuits and, in turn, alterations that influence the way in which the child perceives, analyzes, and responds to the information received.

They usually show difficulties in detecting the most relevant information at all times, problems organizing information and responding in an orderly manner in each situation.

What is the best treatment for ADHD? We mention some of the most proven and effective alternatives.

Psychological Treatment

Educational interventions aim to make the child aware of the limitations caused by the condition and the change it will produce in their daily life, as well as the care they will require.

The main problems that children present are related to the difficulty to meet objectives and maintain adequate performance, both academic and work, as well as developing satisfactory interpersonal relationships, all of which will end up affecting their self-esteem.

The advantage is that these situations can be worked on in individual therapy or through family approaches that allow the family to develop adequate strategies to manage complex patients. You can choose between cognitive-behavioral and interpersonal therapies versus psychodynamic ones, although, in general, multimodal treatments are the most used and effective.

The effect of psychological intervention is indisputable when symptoms of anxiety or depression are detected, but in children who do not show emotional disorders, psychological treatment is not always as successful as expected. This is because the psychological therapies for ADHD in children and adolescents are many and varied, but only a few have been shown to be effective.

The sum of all therapeutic strategies in ADHD in which psychopharmacology is not involved is called psychosocial intervention. The multimodal treatment in ADHD that is part of this indicates the need for interventions from different therapeutic modalities and by different professionals.

The psychosocial intervention comprises a set of programs that have demonstrated their effectiveness in resolving the problems that accompany this condition, since, in addition to addressing regularly identified symptoms, such as inattention, hyperactivity, and impulsivity; it also works on secondary symptoms, such as decreased school performance, behavior problems, and decreased social and relational skills.

This psychosocial approach includes activities that allow an improvement in the attention mechanism and in school performance that help to establish a behavioral expression according to the needs.

Frequently, the diagnosis of ADHD is associated with oppositional defiant disorder, learning difficulties, and affective environment problems due to demotivation and low self-esteem, which entails the existence of so many difficulties on a day-to-day basis.

In this context, it has become necessary to develop psychosocial intervention programs and include actions aimed at reducing the probability of the appearance of comorbid disorders or reducing the intensity of symptoms.

Behavioral Treatment

These are interventions aimed at changing behavior, using social learning and other cognitive theories. It focuses on assessing the child's problem behaviors, determining what stimulates the child to change, and deciding what changes might be most helpful. It is especially useful in children with behavior problems and is less effective in adolescents and adults in general.

This type of treatment is difficult to implement because of the difficulty in selecting rewards and punishments and the tendency of parents to blame each other. Parents often require psychological support.

In young children, behavioral therapy requires that the therapist, with the help of parents and teachers, follow guidelines and instructions. When they understand what are the actions that deteriorate their personal development and relationships with others, they can modify them with less effort.

For this, problem-solving strategies or training in social skills are used. It is the only non-pharmacological intervention that shows significant benefits, especially if associated with medication when it has positive effects but is insufficient for good symptom control.

Psychological therapy through behavioral strategies should be used early since it is a measure that improves the prognosis and its effectiveness is greater in schoolchildren than in adolescents, and when behavioral problems are beginning.

Before beginning behavioral treatment, a behavior log should be established to identify the characteristics of the problems. It can be prepared by parents, educators, or guardians and must specify:

- The characteristics of anomalous behavior and all its important particularities.
- The intensity of the symptoms, including their consistency and their frequency.
- The expression of symptoms in relation to the environment and in which situations worsen or improve.
- Evolution over time.

When problematic behaviors are identified, the strategies to be used are planned, which present as the most important characteristics:

- Behavior modification techniques must be applied continuously. You cannot establish breaks, since they suppose a regression in the achievements.
- Careful coordination of the guidelines used is necessary to apply them in all settings. It is useless for a technique to be applied in one place and not in another, so all those involved must be informed.
- There are no universal intervention programs. The child's problems must be evaluated individually, prioritizing actions on the most important problems.
- It must be taken into account that we are learning, not punishing. Always clarify to the child that we discipline them and that it does not mean that we do not have affection for them.

Those in charge of applying behavioral techniques are the tutors, teachers, and, of course, the child's parents. Work must be done to recognize and identify the problems that appear and the suitability of applying each technique.

Psychological strategies must be used in all contexts, so in addition to family learning, useful guidelines must be provided to educators and teachers. In the intervention, environmental factors, such as socioeconomic and cultural aspects, should not be forgotten. Neither are the factors inherent to the child, such as temperament or maturational level.

Behavioral psychotherapy includes a series of techniques that are relatively easy to apply and to be used in a small setting. The pediatrician must be familiar with them since they are very useful tools from the appearance of the first symptoms. There are valuable behavioral techniques in negotiation and mediation for conflict resolution, which arise in behavioral disorders and others whose objective is to modify problematic behaviors.

Some of the most important are:

Reinforcers or Rewards

Reinforcers are an event or elements that are associated with good behavior to increase the probability of its appearance. For example, if a child fights daily with other children in class and one day they do not fight, then the reinforcer, which could be tangible, will be used as a small gift associated with positive behavior; or intangibles, praise or caress.

Achievement Calendar

Use reinforcers or rewards by recording the child's positive behaviors on a calendar. Each positive behavior carries a signal and when a certain number of signals is exceeded, a prize is given, which can be one of those mentioned in the previous section. The type of prize and the number of signals necessary to obtain it must be previously agreed upon.

Punishments

Children with ADHD easily get used to punishment. Using them should be reserved for significant disruptive behaviors. To apply them it is important to take into account:

- Infrequent and short duration. As we already said, they can get used to it and completely lose their restorative effect.
- It is formulated without disqualifying adjectives about the person. Avoid as much as possible undermining the confidence of the little ones about themselves and what they do.
- An emotional component must be added when communicating the punishment. Explaining why and the consequences that they have on others will help them understand the seriousness of the matter.

EXTINGUISHING TECHNIQUE

It is used when there are intrusive or explosive episodes that cause conflict situations with educators or family members. For its application, the problematic behavior carried out by the child from the beginning must be ignored.

For example: if the family goes to a restaurant for lunch and the child exhibits ongoing negative and defiant behavior, it should be ignored. The first times that ignorance is used there is an increase in negativism and defiance since the child was used to being the center of attention while now they are not. Little by little, they will realize that their behavior has no effect on others and they will lower the intensity until it disappears completely.

CONTINGENCY CONTRACT TECHNIQUE

A contingency contract is a document that contains the results of a negotiation. It is established in writing after the period in which the educator or family member of the child or adolescent discusses a subject on which there are distant positions.

At the end of the negotiation, the results are reflected in the document and the objectives and concessions that the two parties have made are mentioned. You must also collect the consequences of one of the two parties breaking the contract.

Psychoeducation in ADHD

The psychoeducational intervention is a strategy that allows providing the best information on ADHD to the patient, parents, and educators with criteria of usefulness and scientific veracity.

The information about ADHD that is provided to the child should serve to clarify the most important aspects of the disorder and clarify possible preconceived ideas about it. Some points to highlight are:

- Educational styles or teaching patterns do not intervene in

the etiology of ADHD, although these may qualify the expression of symptoms or the severity of the clinical picture.
- The symptoms of ADHD are not developed by the patient voluntarily. It is a disorder of neurobiological origin.
- The diagnosis is clinical. No additional tests or exams are necessary.
- The intervention and treatment must be planned and developed from the diagnosis. It should not be waited, since a delay worsens the prognosis and increases the risk of co-morbidity.
- ADHD can be addressed from Primary Care and should be referred to other specialists when the clinical situation requires it.

There are many resources on the internet that allow for improving knowledge about the disorder, some specific for patients, parents, and educators. There are also manuals on ADHD and patient associations carry out important information and dissemination work.

Routines in daily life help improve organization and planning. The established times for getting up, meals, leisure, school homework and going to bed must be followed as much as possible. Also that the place of study and the physical environment is stable.

The limitation of stimuli decreases the probability of interference in activities that require mental effort. Thus, noise or an abundance of toys must be controlled when it is intended to maintain attention in carrying out school tasks.

At school, they must be seated near the teacher with constant references to what is requested of them, through frequent repetitions by the teacher or with written notes that they can see at all times.

Cognitive Training

Studies evaluating these interventions find few benefits in their use. These are exercises aimed at strengthening working memory, attention, and other cognitive functions. Doing tasks that enhance the performance of what is impaired in ADHD is like exercising to strengthen weaker muscles.

School Support

When there are learning difficulties, a pedagogical treatment of teaching altered academic skills and competencies is essential, and if the impact is very important, schools should carry out specific adaptations to help them in the classroom.

An individualized program must be established to resolve or mitigate the difficulties that may appear in the school setting. Programs may include classroom accommodations, teacher training, behavior modification techniques, enforcement of rules and limits, homework submission, ADHD student assessment systems, and more.

What do children with ADHD want and need?

- Adaptations of the evaluation techniques that are very easy to apply and cost zero, which do not directly affect the elements of the official academic curriculum. This is done in order to adequately respond to the specific educational needs that students with ADHD may present. It is important to structure and tailor truly effective learning tests for each individual.
- Guidelines to improve attention—establish eye contact and approach the child. It is convenient for the student to be seated close to the teacher and away from distractions.
- Guidelines to improve comprehension—use clear and simple instructions. It must be verified that the student understands what the teacher has stated and is allowed to ask questions.
- Guidelines for daily work—the possibility of using other means to present work using computers, diagrams, and drawings. Underline keywords or instructions with markers. Performance improves when extra time is given for written assignments. A rough draft may be made before final grading.

Other Treatments

Multiple treatments of debatable efficacy have been used, from electroencephalographic neuro biofeedback, a kind of self-relaxation controlled by electroencephalogram, to elimination diets, through regulated reading and motility exercises, which are marketed to treat ADHD, some with better results than others and, as we have said throughout this book, should only be applied under the supervision of a professional.

One of the treatments that have shown efficacy is the diet with dietary supplementation with omega-3 essential fatty acids. Studies show that it is effective in different psychiatric disorders, such as unipolar depression, and also in ADHD.

ADHD is a disorder that presents a significant prevalence both in children and adolescents as well as in adults. Currently, the frequency of this diagnosis in all Western countries raises the question of whether an entire generation is being overdiagnosed and overmedicated.

The following are not recommended as treatments for ADHD:

- Diets that eliminate or restrict nutrients without just cause, such as those that eliminate artificial colors.
- Polyunsaturated fatty acid supplements, such as the famous omega-3 and omega-6.
- Vitamin, mineral, or amino acid supplements.
- Herbal products such as ginkgo biloba, ginseng, St. John's wort, valerian.
- Vision therapies, such as eye exercises, perception-behavioral therapy, training glasses, filters, or tinted lenses

Role of the Pediatrician in the Care of the Child With ADHD

We have already talked about the importance of having an experienced professional to guide us in the process with our children. Its main functions are the following:

- Coordinate all therapeutic strategies involved in the multi-modal treatment of ADHD.
- Provide the necessary information on ADHD according to scientific and useful criteria. Appropriate manuals and web pages should be used for this.
- Carry out an adequate initial therapeutic approach through the use of pharmacological and non-pharmacological therapy.
- Control the general adjustment of the child to their environment, establishing the precise recommendations for its achievement.
- Refer families to specialized resources present in the area, such as ADHD patient associations, workshops, forums, and more.
- Adequately advise on treatments that have not shown clinical effectiveness.

ADHD Drugs

We have already explained other times why to use drugs and how to choose the most appropriate for each child. In general, pharmacological treatment is indicated in children older than five years with ADHD symptoms that cause a significant deterioration in their daily activities.

The drug, the doses, and its guidelines must be prescribed by a professional with training and experience in ADHD, who will individualize them for each child and their circumstances. The main medicines have different active principles, whose pharmaceutical forms the specialist must know.

All of these drugs are safe in the short term. Although it is very frequent that they have minor adverse effects, they rarely cause serious adverse effects, which can also be avoided by identifying the patients susceptible to presenting them before starting treatment.

There is no curative treatment for ADHD, but with current procedures and technological advances, 80–90% of patients can improve. First-line treatments, according to the American Academy of Child and Adolescent Psychiatry (AACAP), are methylphenidate, amphetamines, and atomoxetine.

Psychostimulant Drugs

The main representatives of this group are methylphenidate and amphetamines. Despite the fact that there is an important debate about the convenience of using psychostimulants in children and adolescents, their usefulness is beyond doubt, and even more so if there is substance abuse/dependence.

Methylphenidate: The mechanism of action of methylphenidate is the inhibition of brain dopamine transporters, which would slow down the normal process of their reuptake, increasing dopamine at synaptic junctions.

Amphetamine, in addition to using this mechanism, would facilitate the release of dopamine from inside the neurons in which it is stored, so it would be somewhat more useful.

Dopamine would produce an increase in motivation and would facilitate the cerebral response to the execution of tasks. Traditionally, short-acting preparations have been used, which were effective for four to five hours, which meant that school-age children had to ask their teachers to administer the medication one to two times per day.

Traditionally, both methylphenidate and short-acting amphetamine were administered only in the school setting to improve academic performance as well as minimize side effects. Subsequently, it was suggested that ADHD is a disorder that occurs all the time, so treatment was administered throughout the day.

The AACAP recommendation for short-acting methylphenidate is a starting dose of 5 mg twice a day, which may be increased up to a dose of 20 mg for each of the two doses. A third dose may be added at the physician's discretion, depending on the efficacy of the drug; the standard treatment is 3 doses/day, and the maximum dose is 60 mg/day.

Regarding the treatment of ADHD with methylphenidate in adults, the meta-analysis by Faraone et al., which includes six clinical trials with more than 240 patients, confirms that a dose of at least 0.9 mg/kg/day achieves a high (0.9) effect size.

To start treatment, you must first prescribe short-acting drugs, check tolerance and calculate the dose, and only later replace them with delayed-acting ones. Many children and adults, in addition to the morning long-acting tablet, require short-acting supplements in the afternoon, especially if they have significant activity in the evening; they even need several delayed tablets, morning and evening.

Amphetamines: In this group are short-acting amphetamines or mixed salts of amphetamine. The doses recommended by ANPIA are somewhat lower than those of methylphenidate, up to 40 mg/day, divided into 5 mg in each of the two doses initially recommended, with increases of up to 5 mg each week up to a maximum of 20 mg per dose.

There are also long-acting preparations, both dextroamphet-amine and mixed salts of amphetamines. They have been used little in children and adolescents, but there are controlled trials in adults.

Non-Psychostimulant Drugs

Between 20 and 30% of children do not respond to stimulant drugs or do not tolerate their side effects, such as mood swings, anxiety, tics, and others.

Different non-psychostimulant drugs have been used in the treatment of ADHD. Among them, we can identify two large groups: atomoxetine and antidepressants (including bupropi-on, amino oxidase inhibitors, and tricyclics). Other drugs such as nicotinic or guanfacine have also been described, but there is hardly any scientific evidence for their use.

Atomoxetine: It is the only drug recommended by AACAP as first-line, along with methylphenidate and amphetamines, in children and adolescents. On the other hand, it is also the only one accepted by the Food and Drug Administration (FDA) with this indication in adults.

It is not a stimulant and therefore does not cause abuse. It does not act on dopamine but is a selective norepinephrine reuptake inhibitor. The main side effects of atomoxetine are drowsiness and stomach pain, especially if taken on an empty stomach.

There are clinical trials that demonstrate its efficacy: when measured as a 30% decrease in baseline ADHD symptoms, it achieves remission rates of 52% compared to 9% for a placebo.

Antidepressants

Bupropion is a noradrenergic and dopaminergic antidepressant, which has shown efficacy in both children and adults. In children, initial doses of 37.5 mg/day are recommended, which are increased every three to four days until reaching maximum doses of 300 mg/day; in adolescents, 400 mg/day, and in adults, 450 mg/day; in general, it is well tolerated.

Tricyclic antidepressants used for the treatment of ADHD have been nortriptyline and desipramine. They are effective in treating hyperactive and impulsive symptoms but are less effective for inattention than stimulants. They are considered to be especially useful in patients with ADHD who have associated depression, anxiety, oppositional, or tics.

The recommended doses are 25 mg/day, gradually increasing to a maximum of 5 mg/kg/day, except for nortriptyline, which should be limited to 2 mg/kg/day. The treatment takes two to five weeks to take effect and the main side effects are the usual ones with these drugs: dry mouth, constipation, weight gain, sedation, and dysfunction.

Nortriptyline has fewer side effects. The biggest problem in this group is the low therapeutic margin of the drug, with the risk of death due to accidental ingestion or suicidal intent. In adults, desipramine has a clinical trial in which it shows a good therapeutic response.

CONCLUSIONS

Finally, and after a long journey through several chapters, it is necessary to leave other general recommendations that can be used from this moment on in the environment of your child with ADHD, and they are:

- Once you know about your child's condition, it is important that you provide them with an orderly way of life, organizing their schedule and establishing periods for recreation and physical exercise.
- Together establish routines in what you like least.
- Try to divide your tasks from now on into short periods of time, with breaks and constant reinforcement of what has been achieved.
- Establish a time limit after which everyone is released from their task.
- Give them guidelines to pay attention to the fundamental aspects of what they are doing.
- In moments of crisis, do not let yourself be carried away by an angry situation to its extreme. Try to defuse the situation and later, when it's over, reflect together.
- Adapt your learning to your abilities: from structuring home-work to promoting activities in which you stand out.
- Strive to continually find their strengths and avoid continu-ally judging what they do.
- Continually praise them on what they do well, even if it's something that doesn't seem very big or is expected of them.
- Avoid continuous criticism in the family environment.
- Take time to share with your child an activity that they like. If they are older, talk about how they feel, what they think, and what worries them. It is their time, exclusively for them.
- Make it very clear to them that you care about them, that you love them, and that you believe in them.
- Reinforces eye contact during communication, strengthens the bond, and improves the quality of communication.

- Your rules will be followed better if they are clear. Sometimes they don't comply with them because they don't understand them or simply because they don't know them. Explain them.
- Your instructions will be better understood if they are direct, concise, and clear. Avoid being charged with emotion, choose to use a better one with a neutral tone of voice.
- Pay no attention to them when they interrupt and make it obvious when they are allowed to intervene and praise them when they do so at the right time.
- Try to ignore their negative behaviors whenever possible.
- Specify the behavior for which you praise them so you can put a label on it that they will remember and use.

Finally, allow yourself to enjoy your son, because as you already know and it has been understood, they are human beings, simply different like many children. Do not allow opinions or stigmas to harm what you can achieve together; they will thank you, and the best thing is that you will have the satisfaction of having done a good job.

Believe it or not, the fact that you have come this far says how great you are as a father and as a human being, since in other cases, many parents, for one reason or another, simply lock themselves away and focus only on what a doctor can provide to them; something that is not bad, but it is about continuing in the constant search for options that improve the conditions of your child with ADHD and the environment in which they live.